Mel Bay's CONTEMPORARY

SLIDE GUITAR

AN INSTRUCTION MANUAL

ritten by ARVID BURMAN SMITH, JR. &
BARBARA McCLINTOCK KOEHLER

ARVID SMITH, BARBARA KOEHLER
Photo by Alice Owens

DEDICATION

OMPASS QUILT, Photo by Jean Martin

COVER PHOTO-JOHNNY HINES, GAINESVILLE, FLA.
Photo by Alice Owens

COMPASS QUILT
Photo by Jean Martin

This book is dedicated to the memory of Blind Willie Johnson who created some of the most evocative spiritual music on record.

A stereo cassette tape of the music in this book is now available. The publisher strongly recommends the use of this cassette tape along with the text to insure accuracy of interpretation and ease in learning.

ACKNOWLEDGEMENTS

Our thanks to the many wonderful people who urged us to completion. First and foremost to our spouses—Deborah and Bill for their patience, guidance and understanding; much appreciation to George Heaps-Nelson (author of Folk and Blues Harmonica) who helped us immeasurably with his sense of humor on rewrites. Special thanks to Leilani Cook and Bruce Howland for their help with layout and copy.

Not to be forgotten—Ted Doras for his inspiration; all our photographers, especially Alice Owens and Bob McClintock; John Morefield for help with rewrite; Joe Hickerson at the Library of Congress for his cooperation; Geri Horne for attractive graphics; Diana Simon for her patient typing and retyping and lastly to Bill Bay of Mel Bay Publications, who made it all possible, despite our frantic phone calls!

PREFACE

The pieces presented in this book are of a genre of guitar music that has come to be called "American Primitive Guitar." This style is becoming increasingly popular among guitar enthusiasts because it is a unique combination of the old and new. Traditional fingerpicking styles along with various tunings are put together with modern (non-folk) chord progressions and melodies to produce strikingly new sounds.

Some of the principle exponents of this style of playing are John Fahey, Leo Kottke, Robbie Bashô, Peter Lang, Fred Gerlach and a whole stable of other instrumentalists on such guitar-oriented record labels as Takoma and Kicking Mule. Their compositions convey an unspeakable essence that cannot be truly translated into mere notes on a page.

I have tried to present these pieces, along with some traditional blues guitar works, as clearly and concisely as possible and hope that you will enjoy learning them.

Let me say here that I am also indebted to the many students that I've taught over the years for their patience and guidance.

Arvid Smith

Several years of watching and hearing Arvid as he went about teaching guitar in our music store near the University of Florida convinced me that his slide arrangements should be made available to everyone. It's been my pleasure to help him get it all together and edited for publication. The tunes are unique and exciting.

Happy slides -

Barbara M. Koehler

TABLE OF CONTENTS

HOUND DOG TAYLOR
Photo by Peter Amft
Courtesy of Alligator Records

CHAPTER I - INTRODUCTION

Slide guitar is most commonly associated with the rural blues, especially the blues of the Mississippi delta. The various devices used—bottleneck, steakbone, medicine bottle, pocket-knife—make possible the intense, stinging whine which is probably the best known characteristic of the delta blues.

In addition to being deservedly popular in their own right, the delta blues are the foundation on which much of our current rock music is based; slide guitar is playing an increasingly important role in such music. Thus, both traditional and modern pieces are included in this book; if you haven't tried the other guy's music maybe now would be a good time to start.

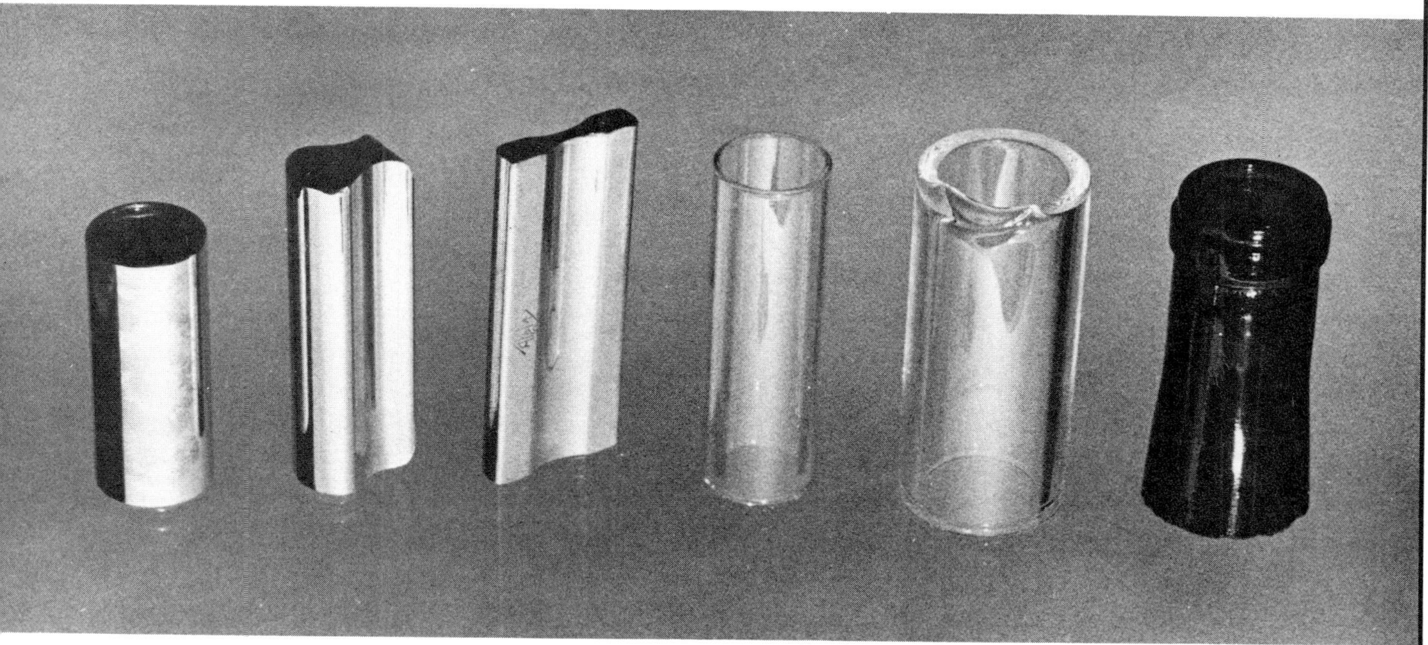

SLIDES, Photo by Alice Owens

A cassette tape with most of the songs from this book is available. The publisher strongly recommends the use of this cassette along with the text to insure accuracy of interpretation and ease in learning.

If the cassette was not included as part of a book/cassette package, it is available from:

SUNNY MOUNTAIN RECORDS, INC.
P.O. Box 14592, Gainesville, FL 32604

or

MEL BAY PUBLICATIONS, INC.
P.O. Box 66, Pacific, MO 63069-0066

WHERE DID SLIDE GUITAR ORIGINATE ?

"A lean loose-jointed Negro had commenced plunking a guitar beside me while I slept. His clothes were rags; his feet peeped out of his shoes. His face had on it some of the sadness of the ages. As he played, he pressed a knife on the strings of the guitar in a manner popularized by Hawaiian guitarists who used steel bars. The effect was unforgettable. His song, too, struck me instantly."

W. C. Handy, **The Father of The Blues.**
1941 MacMillan and Co.
Used with permission.

We can assume from Handy's description of this incident, which took place in Tutwiler, Mississippi in 1903, that slide guitar style was already fully developed. However, the Hawaiian style Handy mentions was not introduced into the United States until 1900; three years would hardly allow time for its full assimilation into southern Negro tradition. We must, therefore, look elsewhere for the origins of this style which has been so prominent in a variety of American musical expressions.

Many well-known blues guitarists had as their first musical instrument a one-string device commonly called the "jitterbug," a single strand of baling wire stretched over two pieces of wood attached either vertically or horizontally to a wall. The artist plucked the string with the right hand while using either a bottle or a pair of pliers to alter the pitch of the string. This instrument is well-known throughout Mississippi and is still played today by both children and adults. Blues artists Big Joe Williams, Bukka White, and Elmore James recall playing an instrument similar to the jitterbug when they were youngsters.

Folklorists have traced this one-string tradition to West Africa, where almost the same techniques have long been used in playing the "musical bow"', which is attached to a gourd resonator and held on the abdomen. The string is plucked and a stick or knife used to vary the pitch. Both the jitterbug and musical bow are closely linked with the bottleneck because inovative traditionalists tended to shift old techniques to new instruments. Bottleneck players use the slide to fret the high strings to different pitches while the thumb of the picking hand plays an even, dronelike bass accompaniment. Many pieces are found in the repertoires of both slide guitar and the jitterbug.

The most telling argument against the Hawaiian theory is that African tradition from which the bottleneck style developed is much older than the Hawaiian style, which was not claimed to have been invented until 1883 to 1895 by a Honolulu schoolboy named Joseph Kekuku. [1] When it was introduced into the United States in 1900 it quickly became popular and probably gave the already-established Negro style further impetus. Folklorist David Evans points out that the bottleneck style was not merely an imitation of the Hawaiian style and that since bottleneck was already developed by 1903, it must have already had a few years to mature. [2] An equally striking argument, says Evans, is that Negros have never played or sung Hawaiian tunes and that it does not seem likely that black musicians would adopt the style but none of the songs. Evans' hypothesis is that Joseph Kekuku possibly got the idea for Hawaiian guitar style from an American Negro sailor whose ship was docked in Honolulu.

The slide guitar styles we hear today, like everything else in folk and popular music, are the result of many years of change and a multitude of influences, so there is no one "right" way to play. Once you learn the basic techniques presented in this book you can adapt them to your own kind of music, whether it be country, rock, or folk blues. The special effects of the slide will enable you to play blues like Handy's friend or rock in the style of Duane Allman.

1 David Evans, **Afro-American One Stringed Instruments.** Used with permission.
2 Ibid.

CHAIN SINGING-LOUISIANA 1934
Photo by Library of Congress Collection

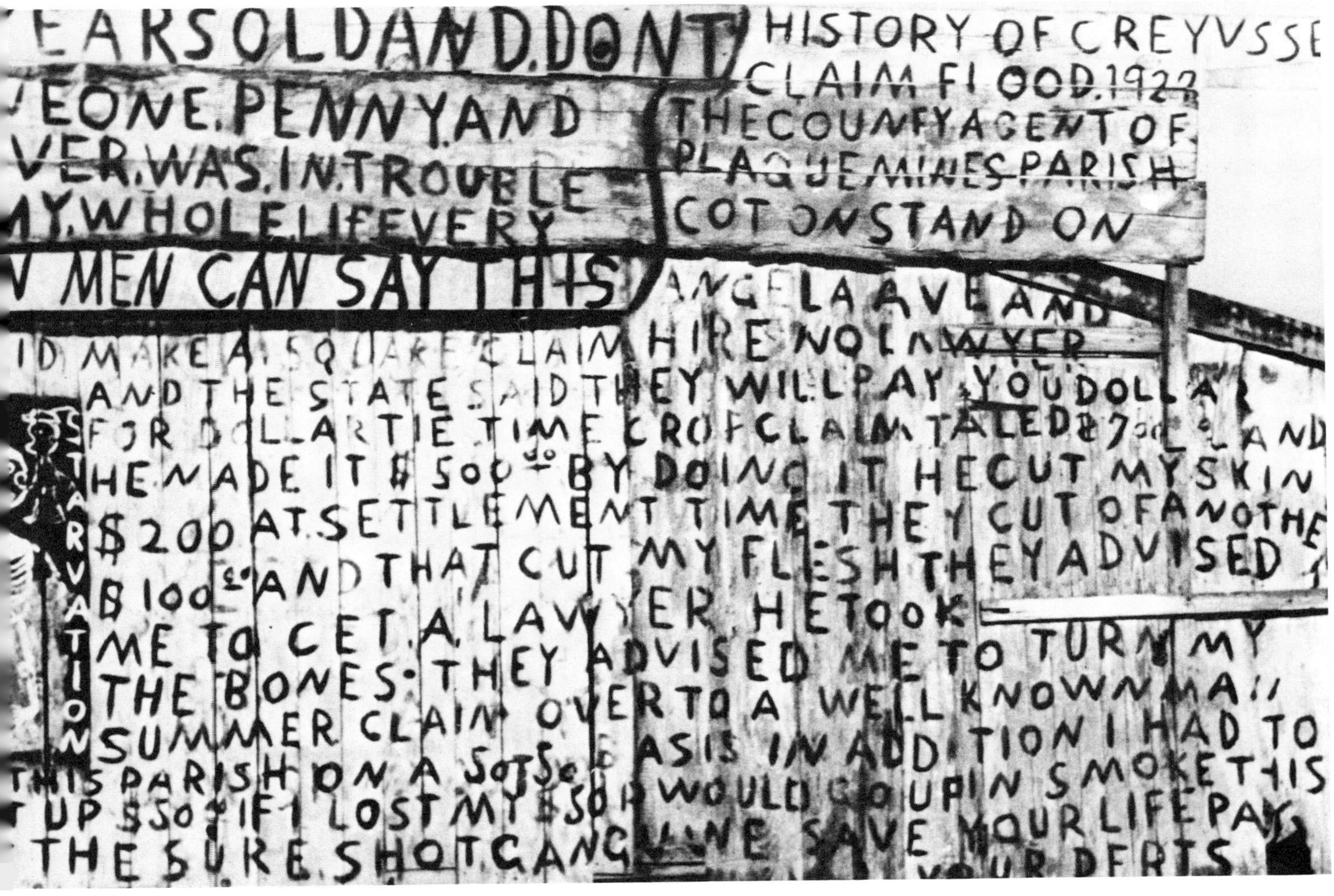

S CAMPAIGN TO OBTAIN 1927 FLOOD DAMAGE PAYMENTS FROM RISH, NEW ORLEANS, VICINITY, 1939.

Photo by L. Block
Library of Congress Collection

WOOD STOVE, Photo by Bob McClintock

THIS OLD ICEBOX LIKE SOME OF THE PEOPLE I SAW, IS FLAKY BUT STILL WORKIN! Photo by Bob McClintock

CHAPTER II
THE TABLATURE SYSTEM

The tablature system is essentially a six line staff with each line representing a string of the guitar. The numbers on top of the lines represent the fret to be played with left hand. The line itself tells you which string is to be played.

The top line is the high (E1) string of the guitar.

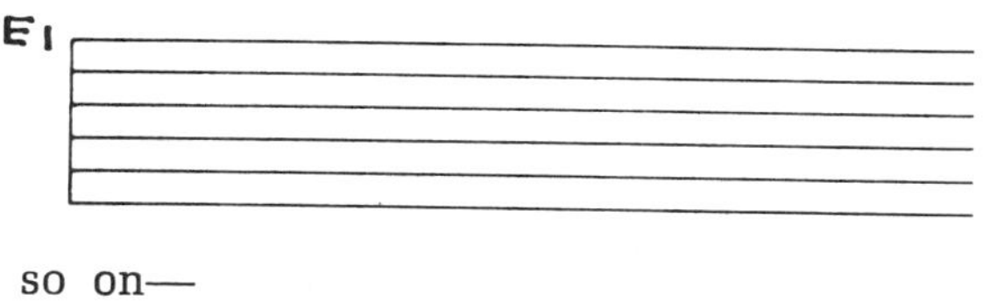

and so on—

So if you see this

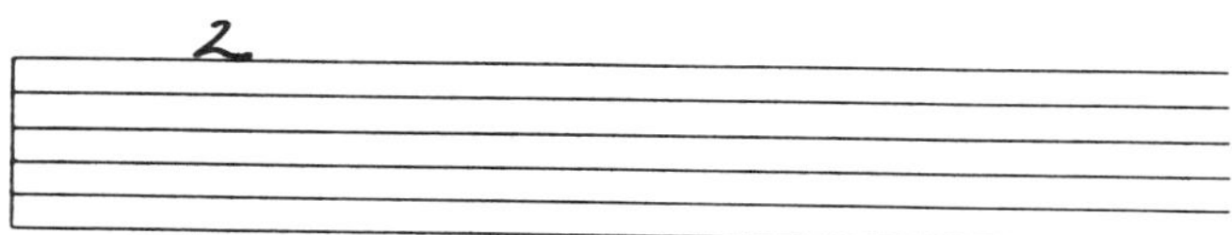

place the first finger of your left hand on the second fret of the 1st string (E1) and pluck the first string with your right hand.

The melody of **London Bridge** (notice that we start out with the heavy stuff) would be notated thus:

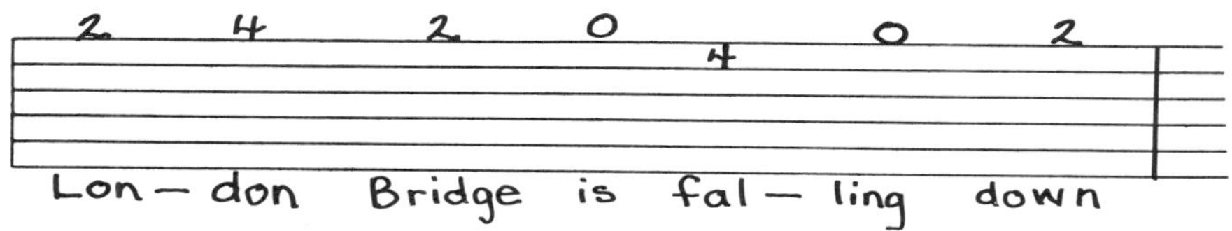

A D chord in this fashion:

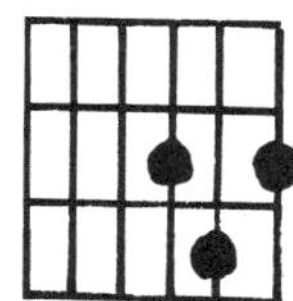

in standard tuning would be notated

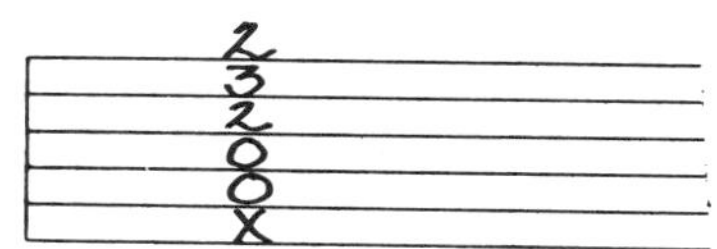

IN EVERY HONEST TO GOODNESS FARMYARD THAT I'VE SEEN IN THE SOUTH THERE IS A CAR LIKE THIS. SOMETIMES IT'S USED AS A FLOWERPOT, SOMETIMES AS A CHICKEN ROOST, SOMETIMES IT'S LEFT AS A MONUMENT TO A LONG FORGOTTEN HONEYMOON.
Photo by Alice Owens

Photo by Bob McClintock

FINGERSTYLE PLAYING

Two basic finger picking patterns are used. The thumb plays an even steady bass while the fingers pick out the upper voice. The two patterns are illustrated here on a C major chord in standard tuning.

Example 1

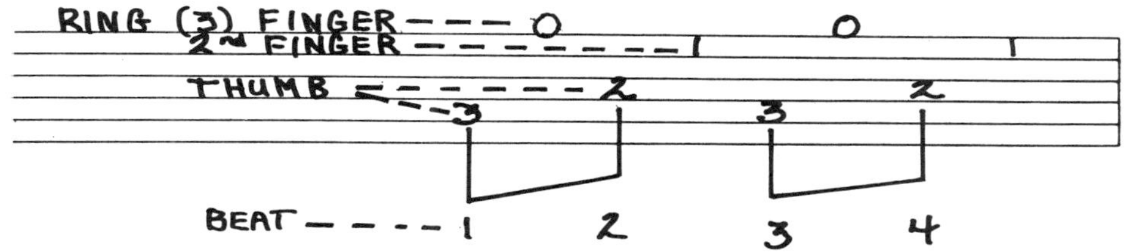

Upper notes are played after each beat.

If an upper note should happen to fall on a third string the index finger would be used for that note.

C

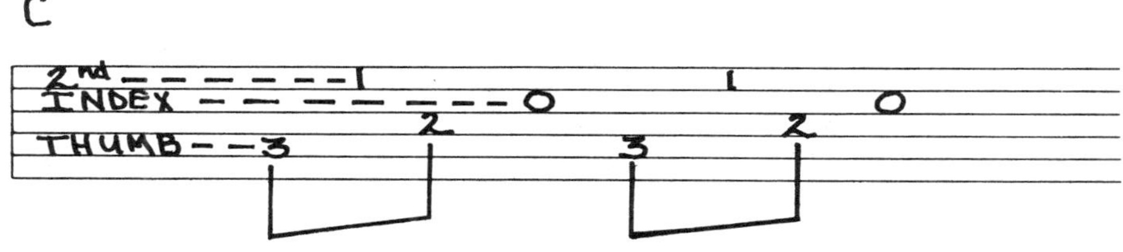

Important! Any notes joined by the brackets └─┘ are to be played with the thumb. As in example one, these carry the beat of the song.

. . . KEEP ON GOIN'

Pattern two is a bit more complex but should give you little trouble.

Example 2

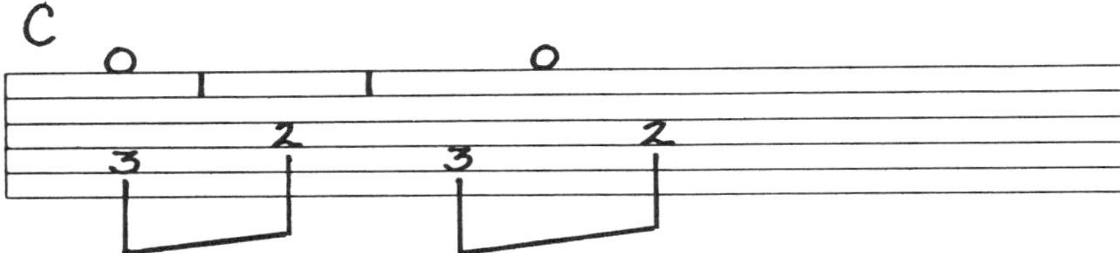

The position of the first string open (directly above fifth string third fret) indicates they are sounded simultaneously. Again, keep the thumb moving in an even steady beat.

Both picking patterns should be practiced continuously as they are used throughout most of the pieces. If you get bored doing this heave a few dramatic sighs and keep at it. You need the practice and it will strengthen your fingers, build your character and make your feet smell sweet.

In many of the pieces a single line melody is played over the bass as in **Oh Papa.** Here all the melody notes are directly over the bass. In other songs the melody notes do not line up. These then are played as in the picking patterns **after** the previous beat.

SATURDAY NIGHT 1939
Photo by R. Lee
Library of Congress Collection

OH PAPA

Arvid Smith

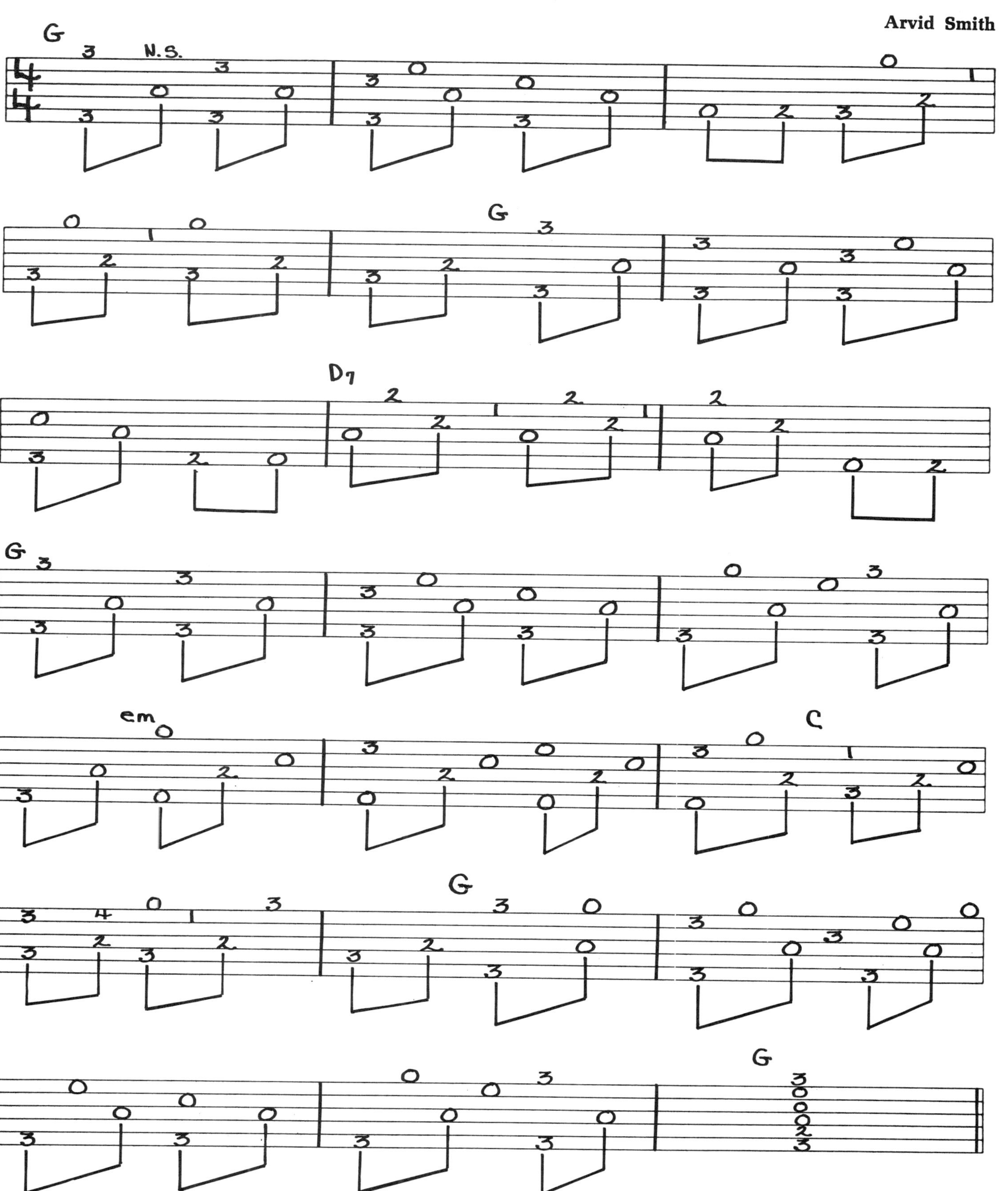

SYMBOLS USED IN THIS BOOK

1. The symbol **H** over two notes indicates a "hammer-on". This is a slurring technique where the right hand plucks the string for the first note and a finger of the left hand quickly presses down the second note without any right hand motion. The second note will always be higher than the first.

2. The symbol **P** over two notes indicates a "pull-off". For this technique the right hand plucks the string to sound the first note and the fretting finger of the left hand then plucks the string to produce the second note. It is the opposite of the "hammer-on" as the second note is always lower than the first.

3. The word **slide** means simply to use the slide for fretting the note, natch. The initials N.S. mean "no slide" and this occurs where the fingers fret the note.

4. A dash between two notes (9——12) indicates that the slide is to stay on the string for the duration of the change of pitch.

5. A squiggle (~~) attached to a note indicates the string is to be "bent" or "choked" to raise the pitch. To bend or choke a note you vary the pitch by a slight push or pull with your fretting hand. I find pushing a whole lot handier because if you pull you can get a horrible buzz on the first string. These notes are always fretted with the finger—not the slide.

WHICH SLIDE IS BEST FOR YOU ?

The slide I prefer is an ordinary glass bottleneck. It should be straight so that it won't interfere with the other strings of the guitar and it should also be long enough to go across all the strings. You'll see why later. The thicker the glass the better. I like the heavy feel because heavier glass seems to give a greater sustain quality and makes for a good vibrato effect. Another advantage is the smooth sound that you just can't seem to get with a metal slide. To get the bottleneck from the bottle in the traditional fashion, tie a kerosene soaked string around the bottle at the point at which you wish the separation to occur, light the string and take advantage of the resulting weakness to get a good clean break. Be careful not to cause an explosion in the process.

There are many commercially manufactured slides available due to the tremendous popularity of slide guitar. They are available in both glass and steel and range in sizes and density from light to heavy. Some of the lighter ones are especially nice for playing electric slide guitar which usually demands a lighter touch than an acoustic instrument.

Some players prefer metal over glass as it gives them a harsher, rougher sound than glass. Son House used a chunk of copper tubing, while Blind Willie Johnson used a knife. Metal is also great for playing electric slide. For lap style a solid metal bar is much easier to handle.

All in all the choice is up to you—experiment with the various types available and see what feels best to you.

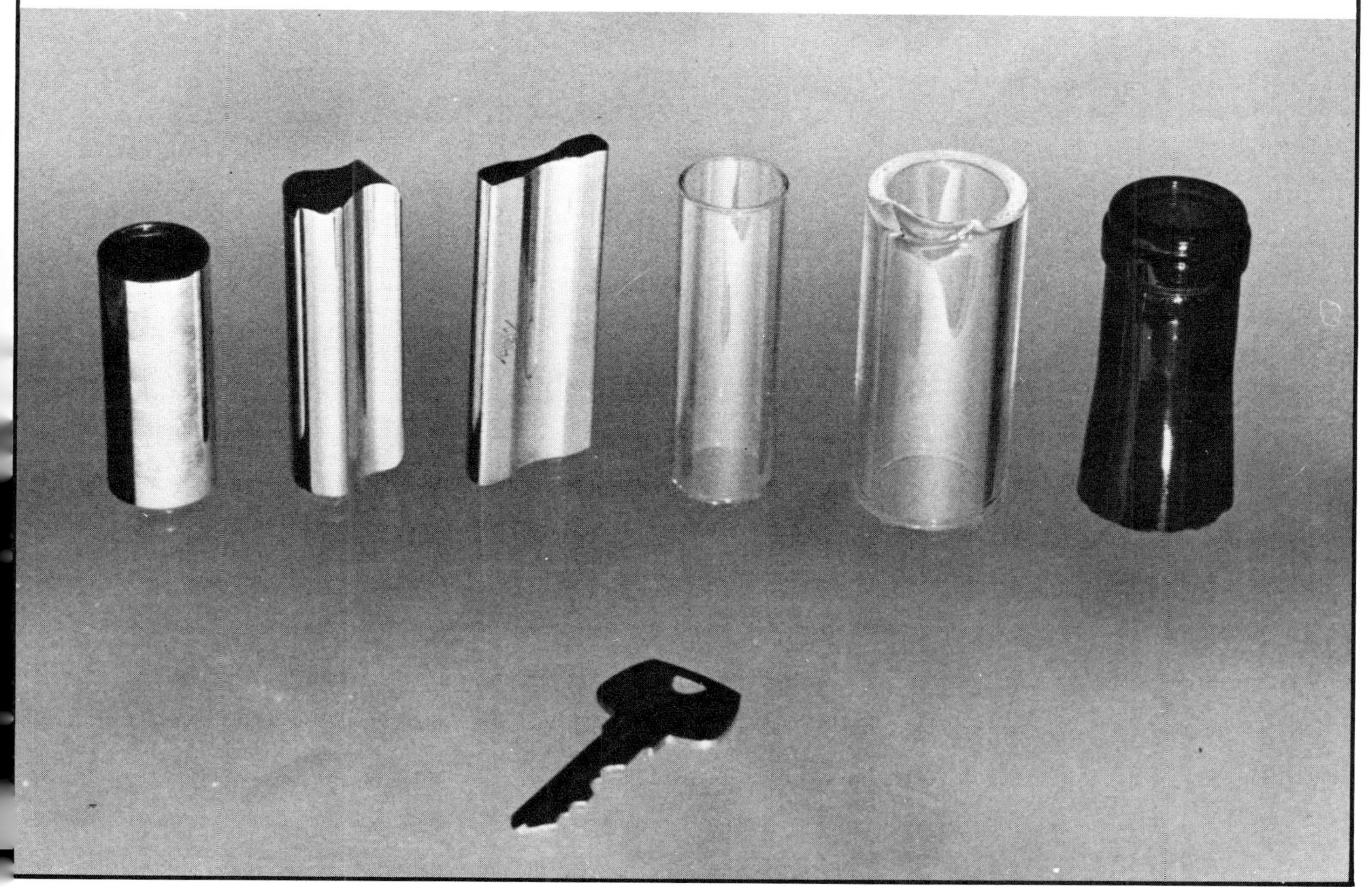

SLIDES, Photo by Alice Owens

HOMEMADE WOOD BURNING STOVE
Photo by Bob McClintock

SLIDE TECHNIQUE

When you get right down to it the slide acts as a movable fret. With this in mind the possibilities for vibrato, sustain, and single line expression are endless. If you don't know these words fake it or look them up.

First, to get the proper sound, just let the slide rest on the string. **Don't** push it down against the fingerboard.

Next, for proper intonation, the slide must be placed directly over the fret. Not in front of it as in normal playing.

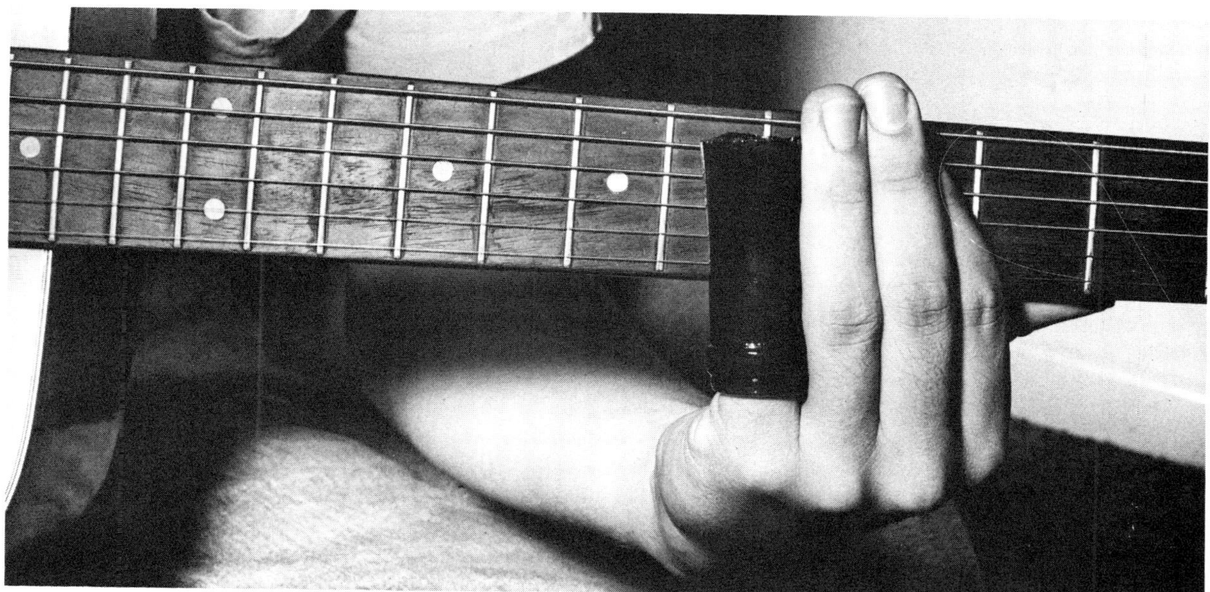

SLIDE POSITION

Photo by Bob McClintock

Try sliding up and down the neck slowly, keeping the slide parallel with the frets. When moving around on the neck remember that your thumb should be kept on the back of the neck. If your thumb is out in front it can cause you to lose control of the slide and get sloppy sounds. Another way to keep your slide from wandering is to keep your fingers all touching one another (something like a left-handed Boy Scout salute). This is especially effective when the slide is across all the strings and moving up or down sounding chords.

Photo, Library of Congress Collection

There's an old guy who roams the back streets of Gainesville. He's old, but somehow his eyes don't show it, and he's always got a new story to tell, "Sure! I remember that big old fire, took 'em near two days to put it out. I only remember one thing 'bout it tho', an' that was a little bitty doll just a-lyin' there that somebody done forgot." But he also tells stories about when he fought Joe Louis. So you never know.

Don't be afraid to experiment around if some of these seem uncomfortable at first. Whatever feels good and gets good sounds is right for you.

Which finger the slide is to worn on is really a matter of personal preference. Many players find it comfortable to wear it on the ring finger. For the songs in this book where the slide frets every note, any finger will do. However, some songs will be combining conventional chord fretting with slide. These songs are designed for the slide to be worn on the little finger. Don't fret, you'll get used to it.

STRING ACTION

A player who uses a guitar with very low action and light gauge strings will probably run into trouble, because the weight of the slide will push light strings against the frets, causing a buzz. So fairly high action (at least 156/1000 inch minimum measuring from the top of the fingerboard to the top of the string at the 12th fret) is best. Medium-light to medium gauge strings will also work better than light or extra-light strings.

However, as your technique and control improve, you should be able to play on any gauge string.

SHARECROPPER FARM-MISSOURI 1938
Photo by R. Lee
Library of Congress Collection

CHAPTER III
OPEN G TUNING

Perhaps the most common tuning for slide guitar is the open G tuning. The notes for the strings from the sixth string through the first string are:

D	G	D	G	B	D
6	5	4	3	2	1

The steps for arriving at open G tuning from standard are:

1. Lower the sixth string (E6) to one octave below the fourth string (D).
2. Lower the fifth string (A) to one octave below the third string (G).
3. Tune the first string (E1) to the note of the second string third fret. This will lower the first string from an E to a D one octave higher than the fourth string.

Standard		Open G
E1	Lowered to	D
B	Same	B
G	Same	G
D	Same	D
A	Lowered to	G
E6	Lowered to	D

G tuning is particularly nice because it gives you strong basses in both G and D and also gives you a tonic note (G) in the middle of your first string.

hoto by Alice Owens

SAVANNAH

Arvid Smith

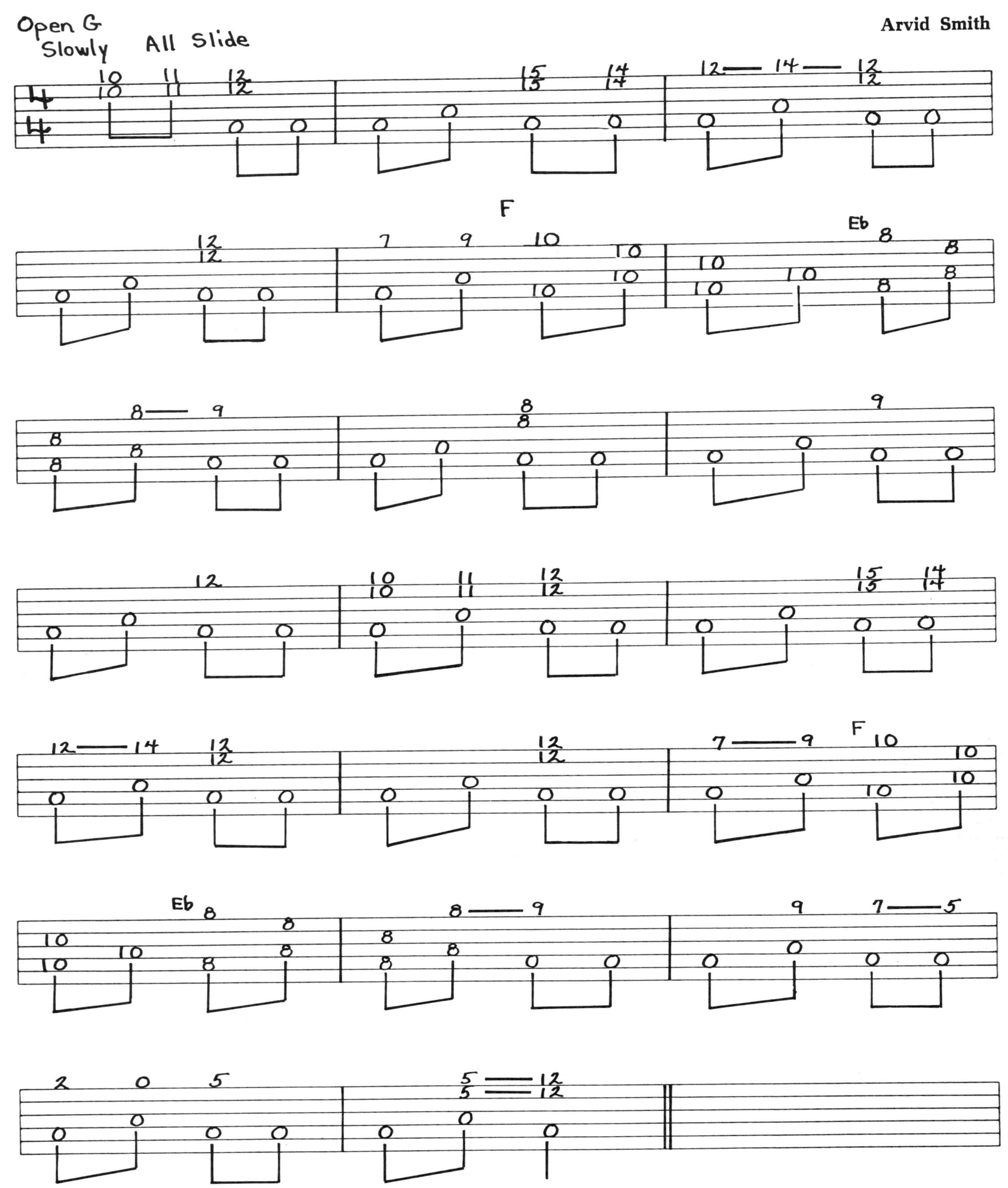

WATERS RISING

Traditional
Adapted by Arvid Smith

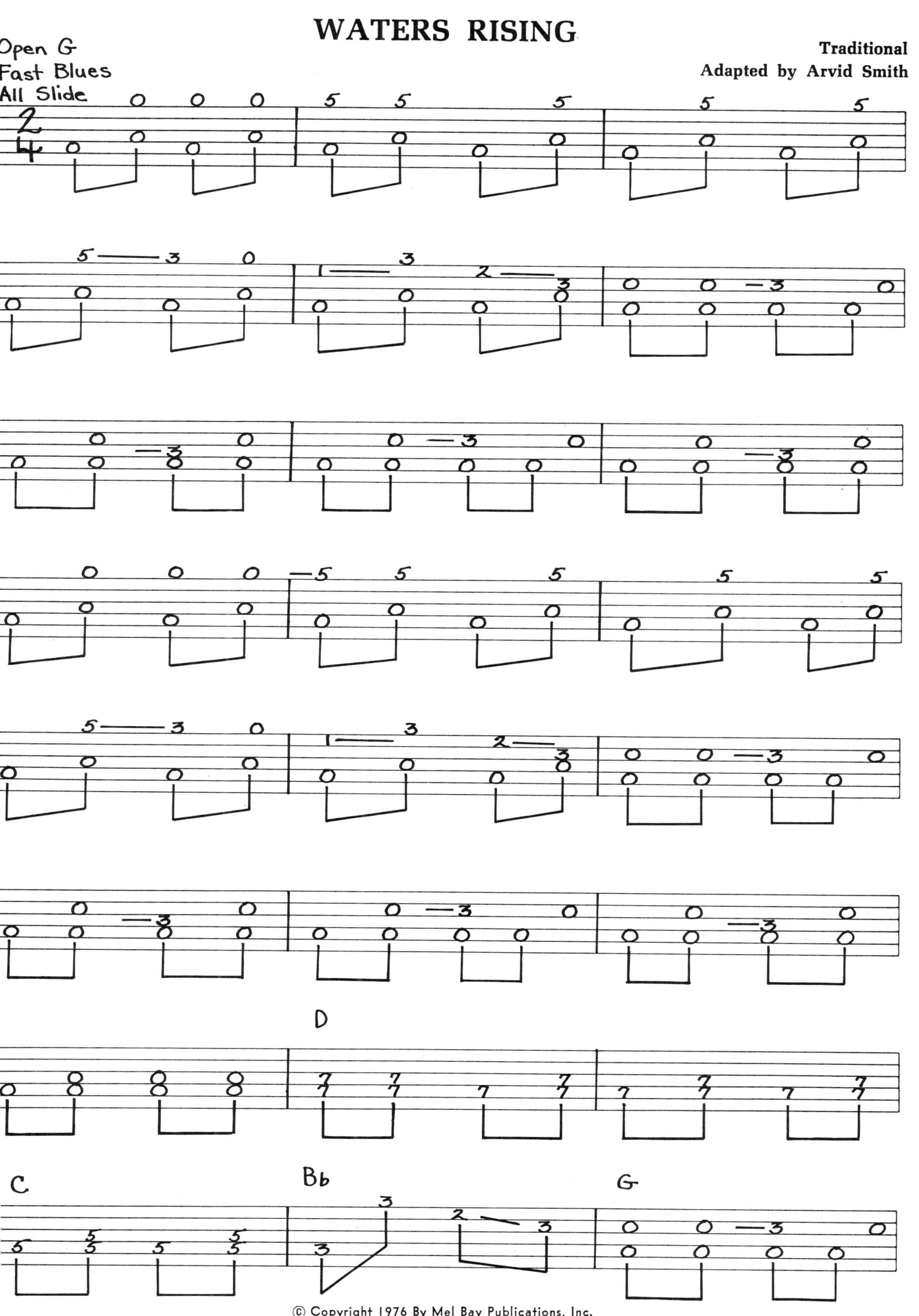

WATERS RISING

WATERS RISING

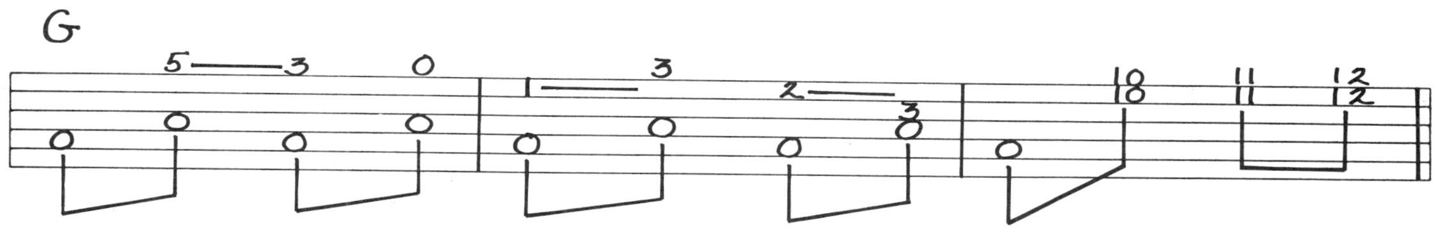

Photo, Library of Congress Collection

Photo by Bob McClintock

Lebanon Station isn't really a railway station at all. It's a pocket hidden somewhere off the highway. All most people ever see of it is a small green sign by the side of the road. To my knowledge, there i only one. It says LEBANON STATION: 64 MILES. But whether it ha fast noisy train streaking through it in the afternoon, or whether the only action it sees is those complete grey Florida thunderclouds rolling across it in the evening, the feeling is the same. It's a feeling th won't leave the small southern towns, or the solitary families that live there, through the sunsets or the storms.

This picture was taken somewhere up in Georgia; it doesn't muc matter where. And this stationmaster is one of a dying species, and h hometown could be Waldo, Florida or Hammond, Louisiana, And the song that follows can be played on any front porch in any place that people who want to play it. The view might be a whole oak grove, or solitary maple up the block. The feeling is the same.

Photo by Bob McClintock

LEBANON STATION

Arvid Smith

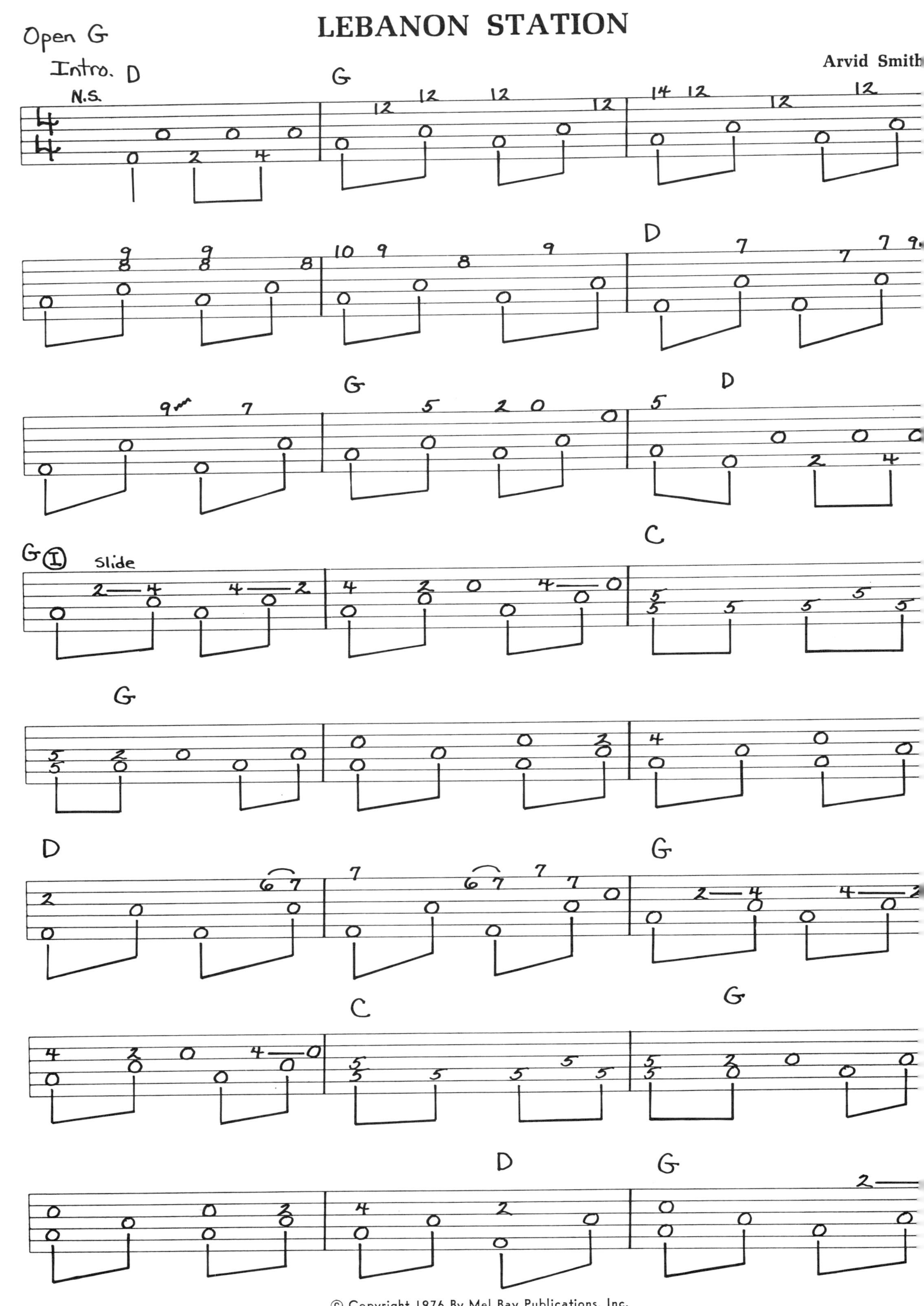

LEBANON STATION

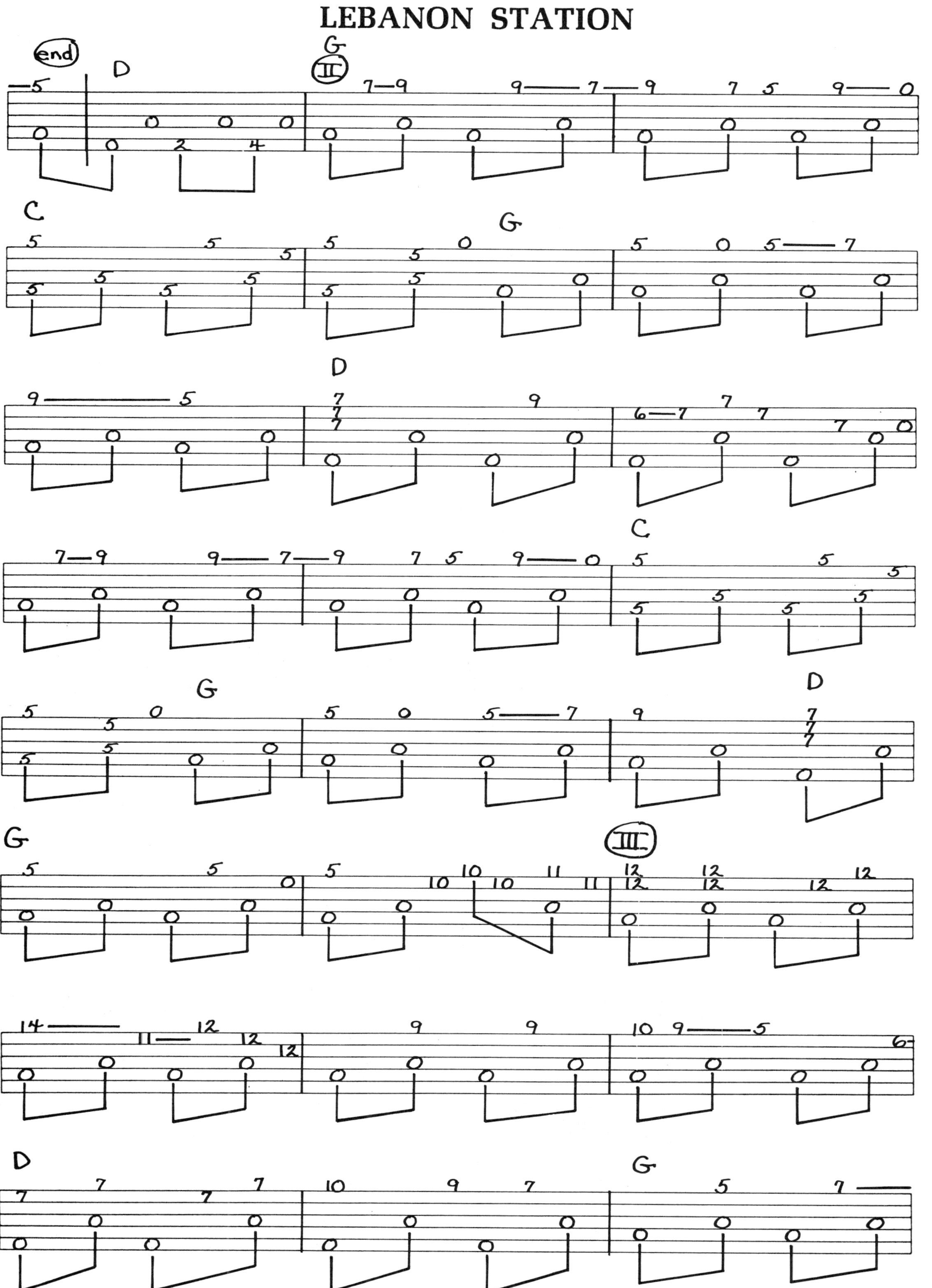

LEBANON STATION

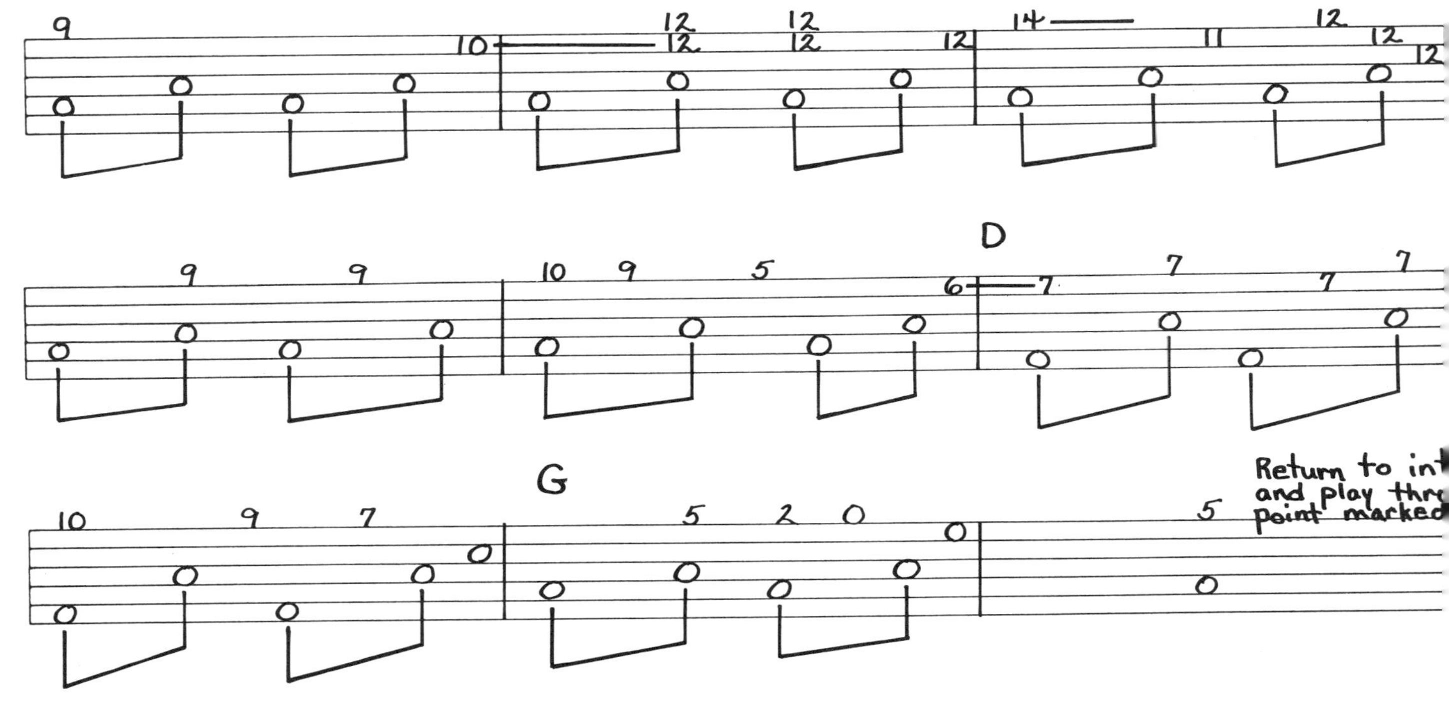

MAYNARDSVILLE, TENN., OCT. 1935
Photo by Shahn
Library of Congress Collection

oto by Bob McClintock

3

UNTITLED 1974

Arvid Smith

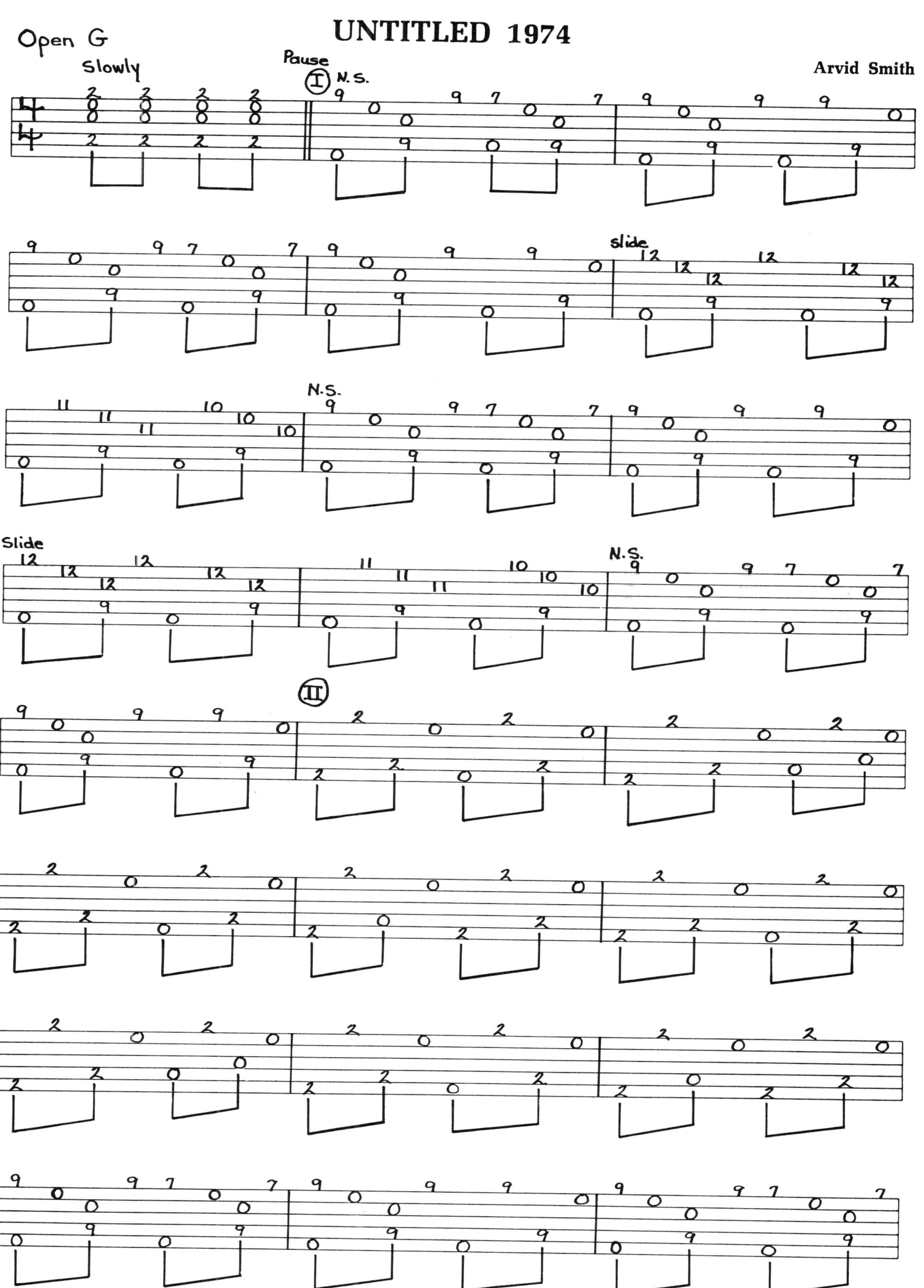

oto by Alice Owens

UNTITLED 1974

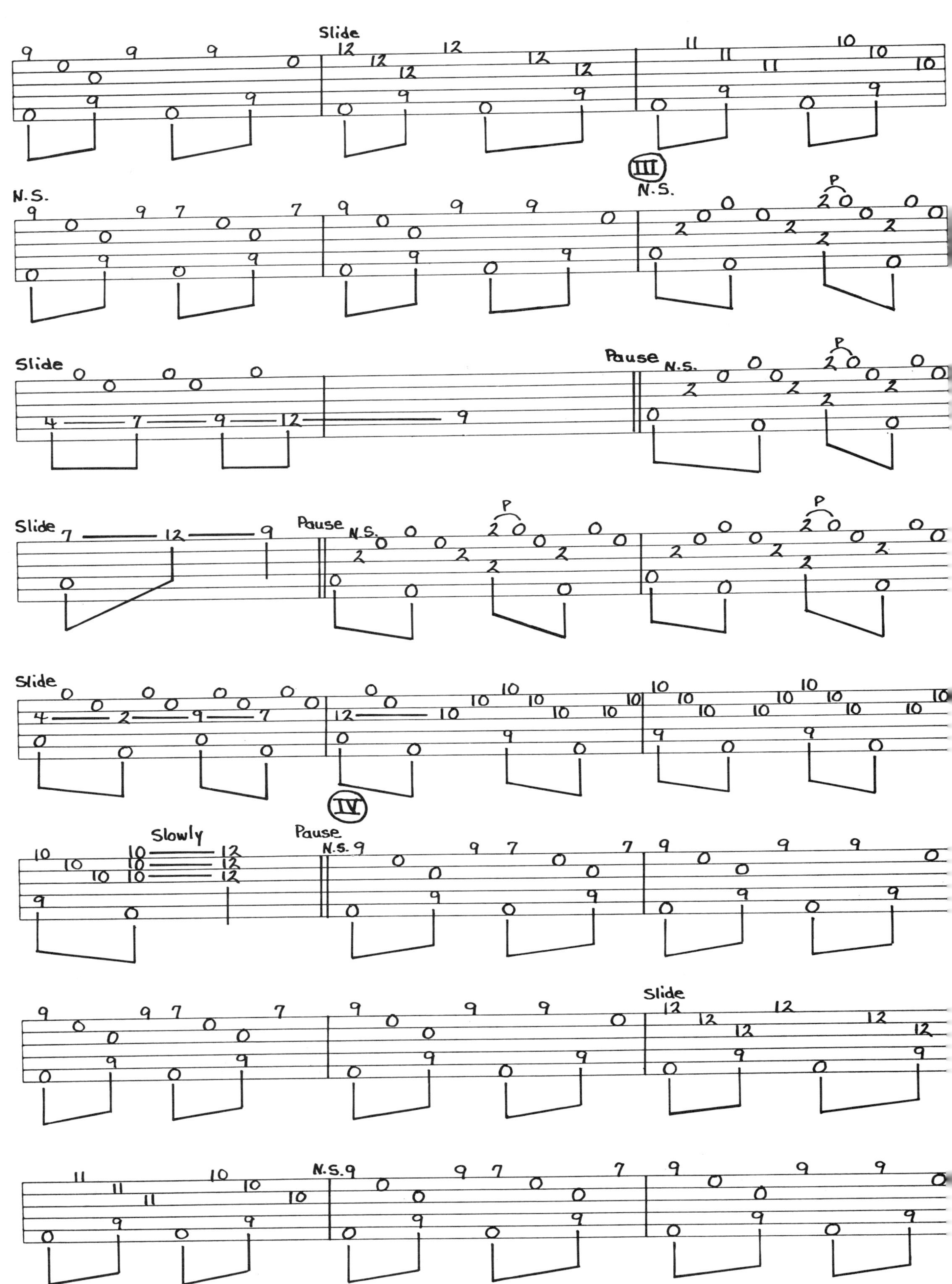

UNTITLED 1974

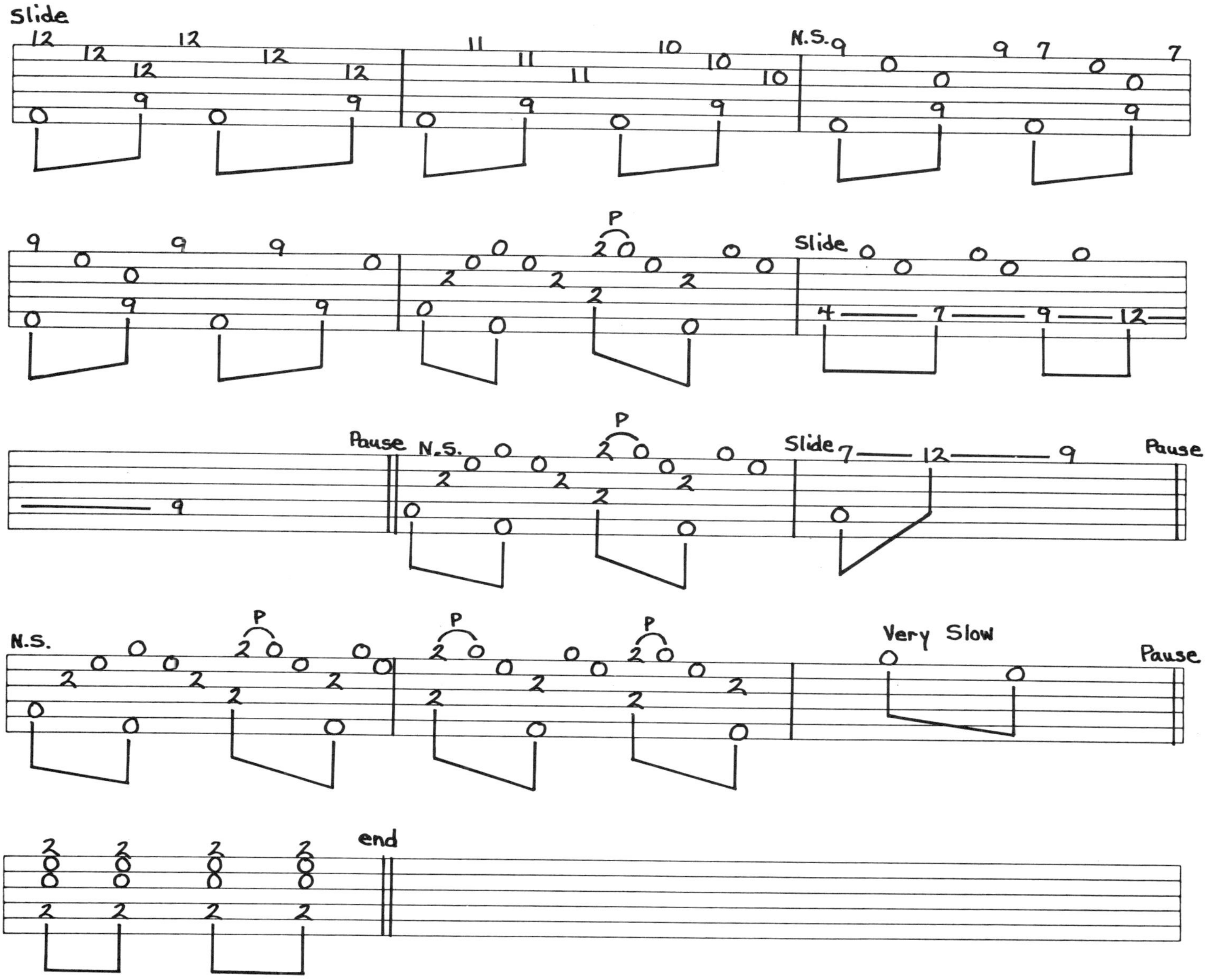

Slide N.S.

Slide

P

Pause N.S. Slide Pause

P

N.S. Very Slow Pause

P P P

end

Photo by Bob McClintock

If you have got these songs down, or maybe if you don't for that matter, listen to Robert Johnson's **Terraplane Blues,** Leo Kottke's **Sailors Grave on the Prairie** and Son House's **Son Goin' Down** (see discography for available albums) which are all played in G tuning.

CHAPTER IV
OPEN G DROPPED C TUNING

This is a homemade tuning. I've heard that Ry Cooder also came up with this tuning but I don't know whether he used it on any of his records. It's basically the same as the open G tuning discussed in the last chapter. The only difference is that the sixth string of the guitar is lowered from a D down to a C. This gives a strong bass bottom for the C chord.

To arrive at this tuning from standard tuning first place the guitar in open G tuning.

Then all you have to do is place a finger on the fifth fret of the fifth string to one octave below that note.

Open G		Dropped C
D	Same	D
B	Same	B
G	Same	G
D	Same	D
G	Same	G
D	Lowered to	C

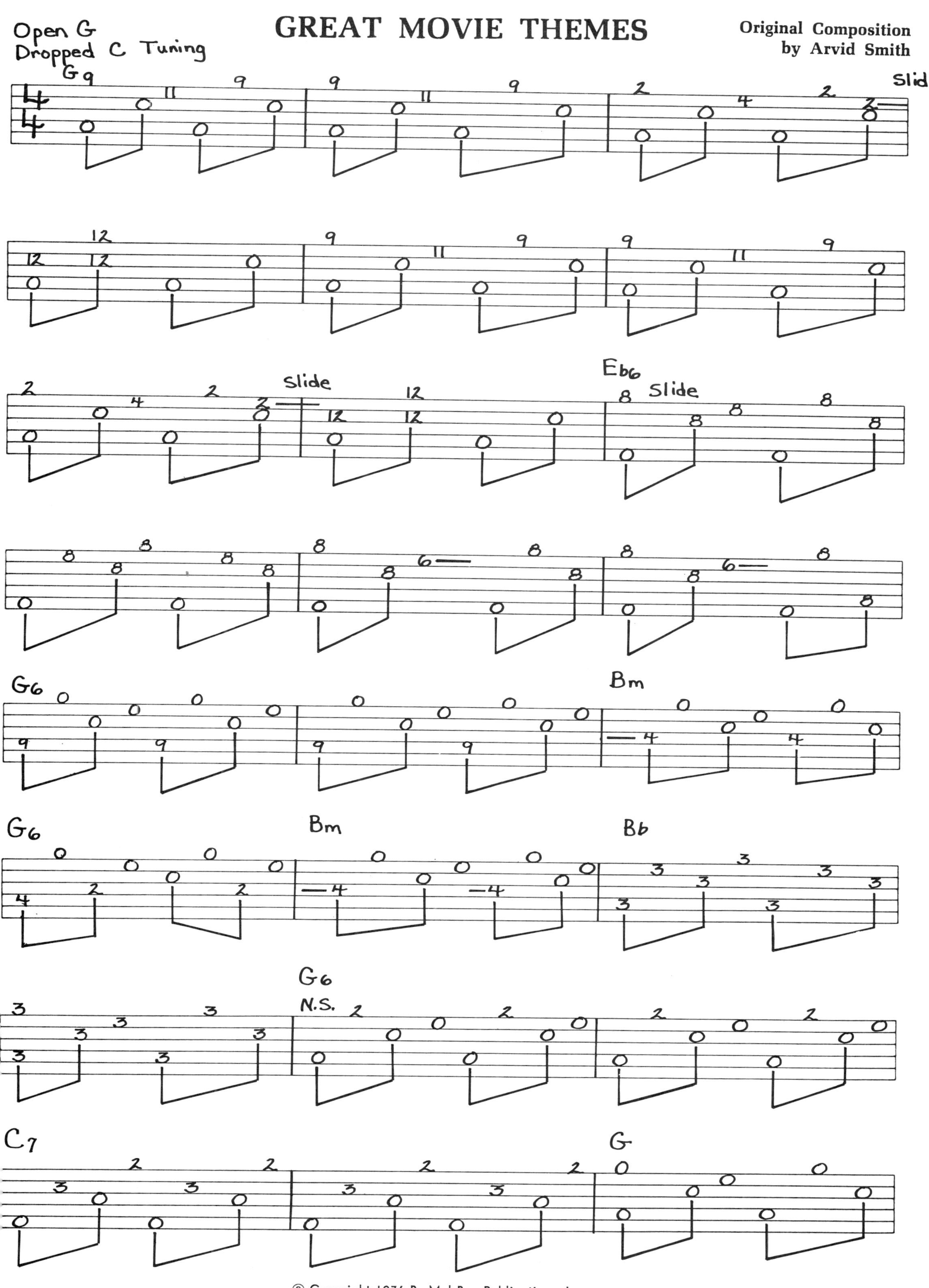
Open G
Dropped C Tuning
GREAT MOVIE THEMES
Original Composition
by Arvid Smith
G9
Slide
Slide
Eb6
Slide
G6
Bm
G6
Bm
Bb
G6
N.S.
C7
G
© Copyright 1976 By Mel Bay Publications, Inc.
International Copyright Secured Printed in U.S.A.
All Rights Reserved

GREAT MOVIE THEMES

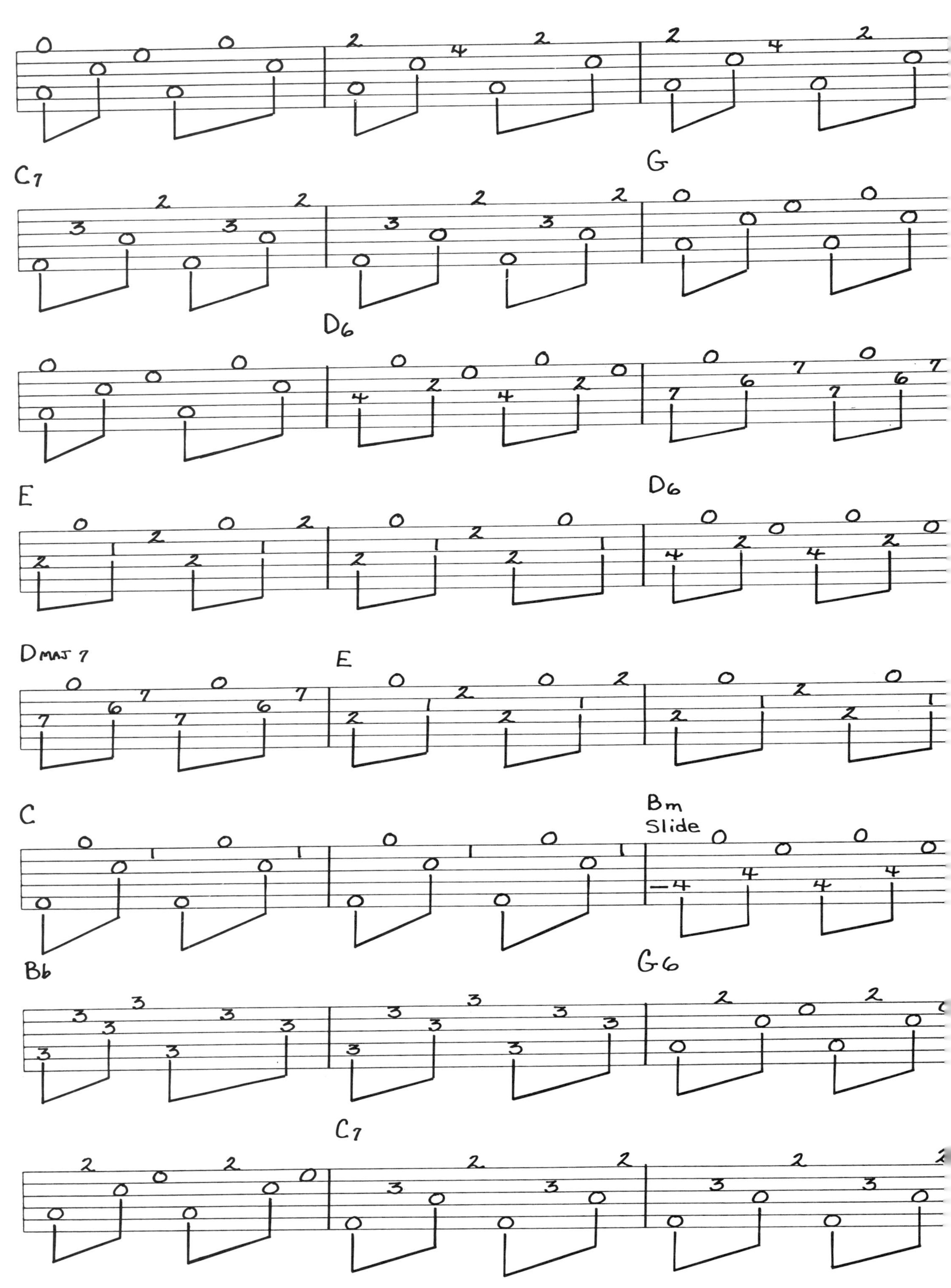

GREAT MOVIE THEMES

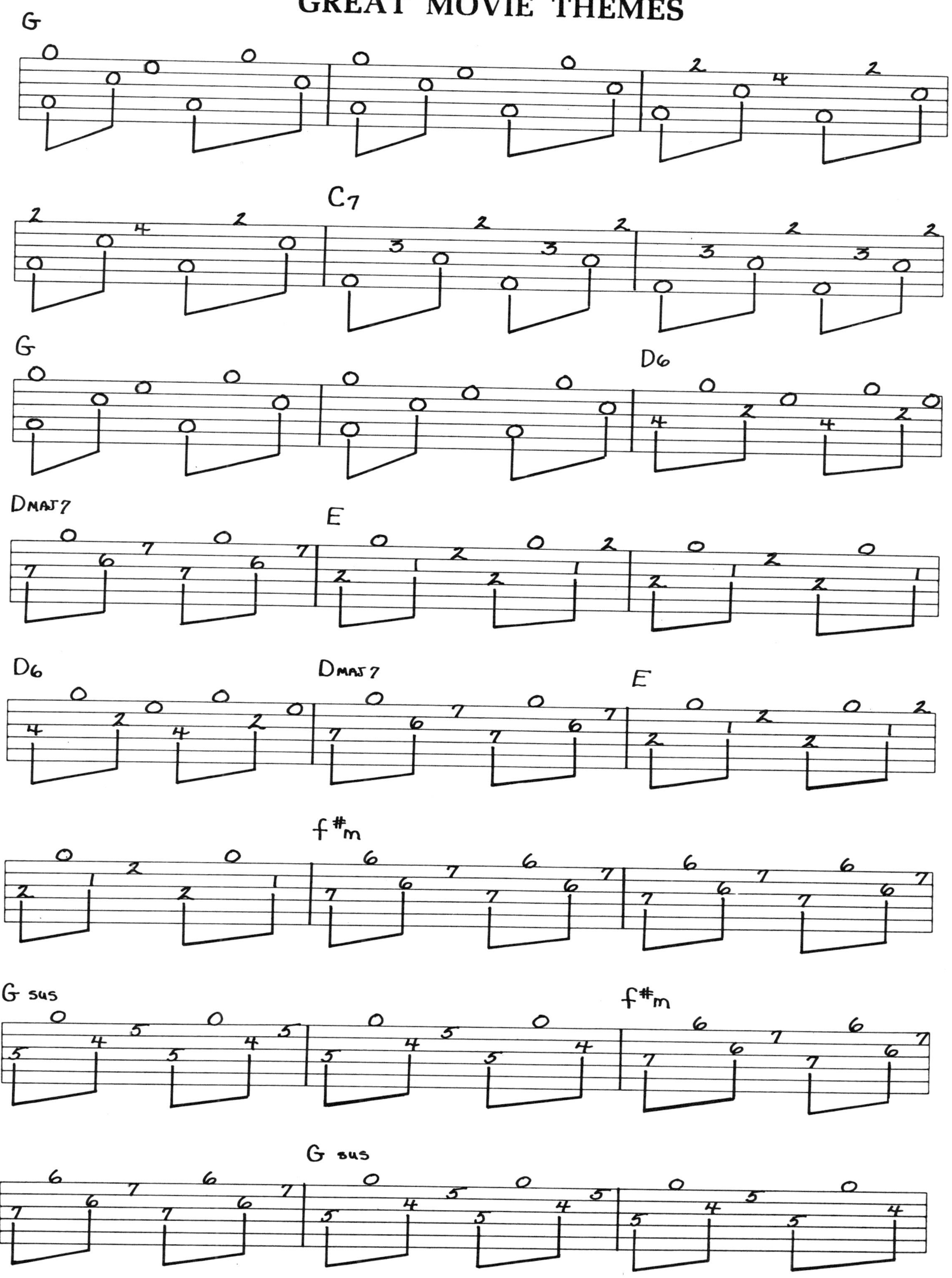

GREAT MOVIE THEMES

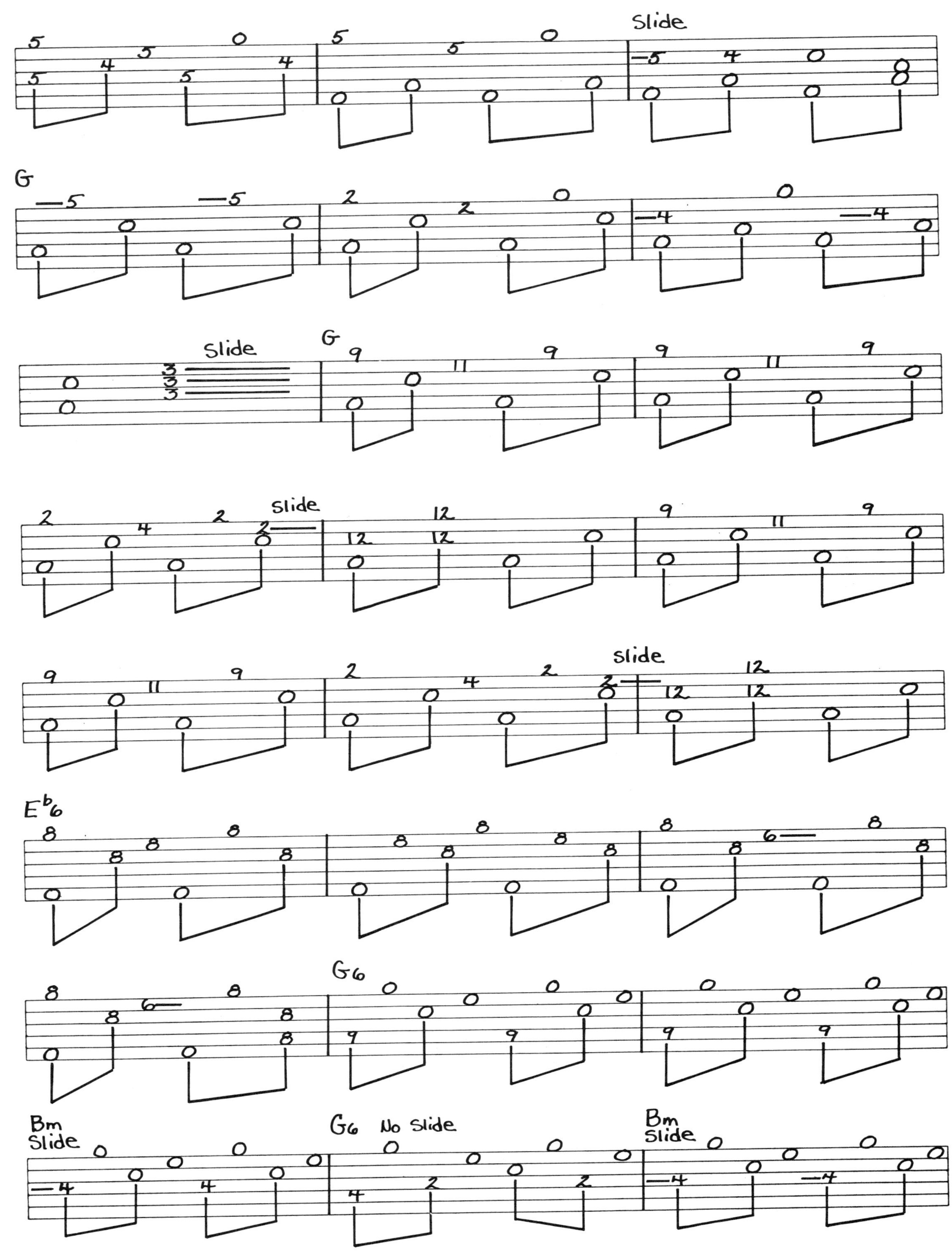

GREAT MOVIE THEMES

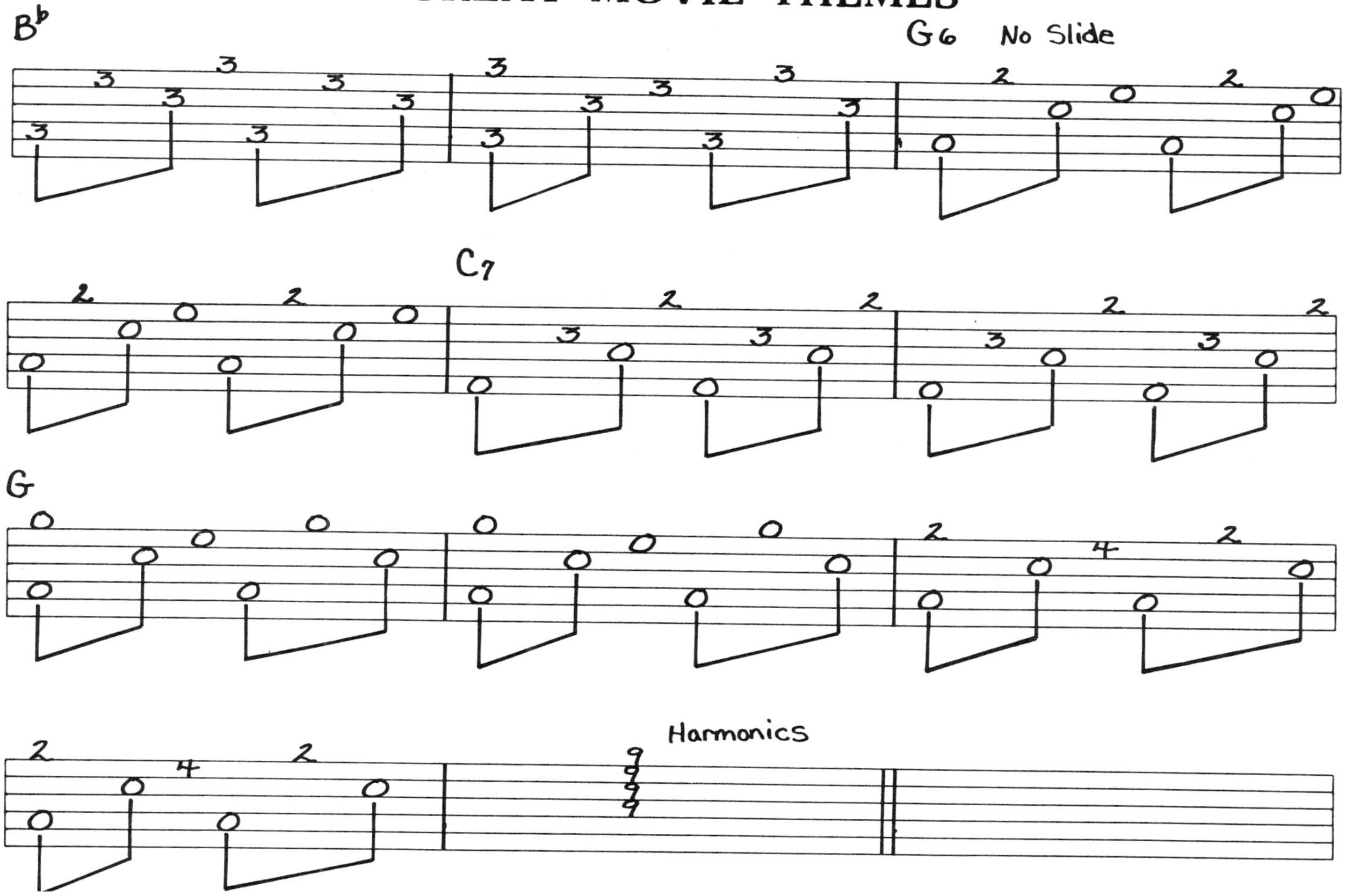
B♭
G6 No Slide
C7
G
Harmonics

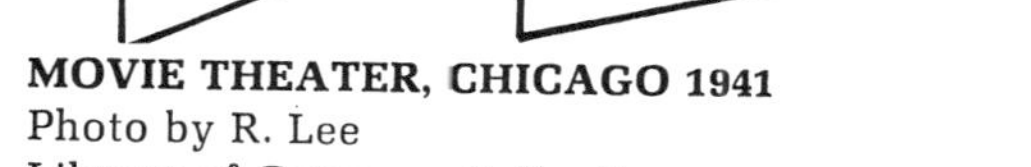

MOVIE THEATER, CHICAGO 1941
Photo by R. Lee
Library of Congress Collection

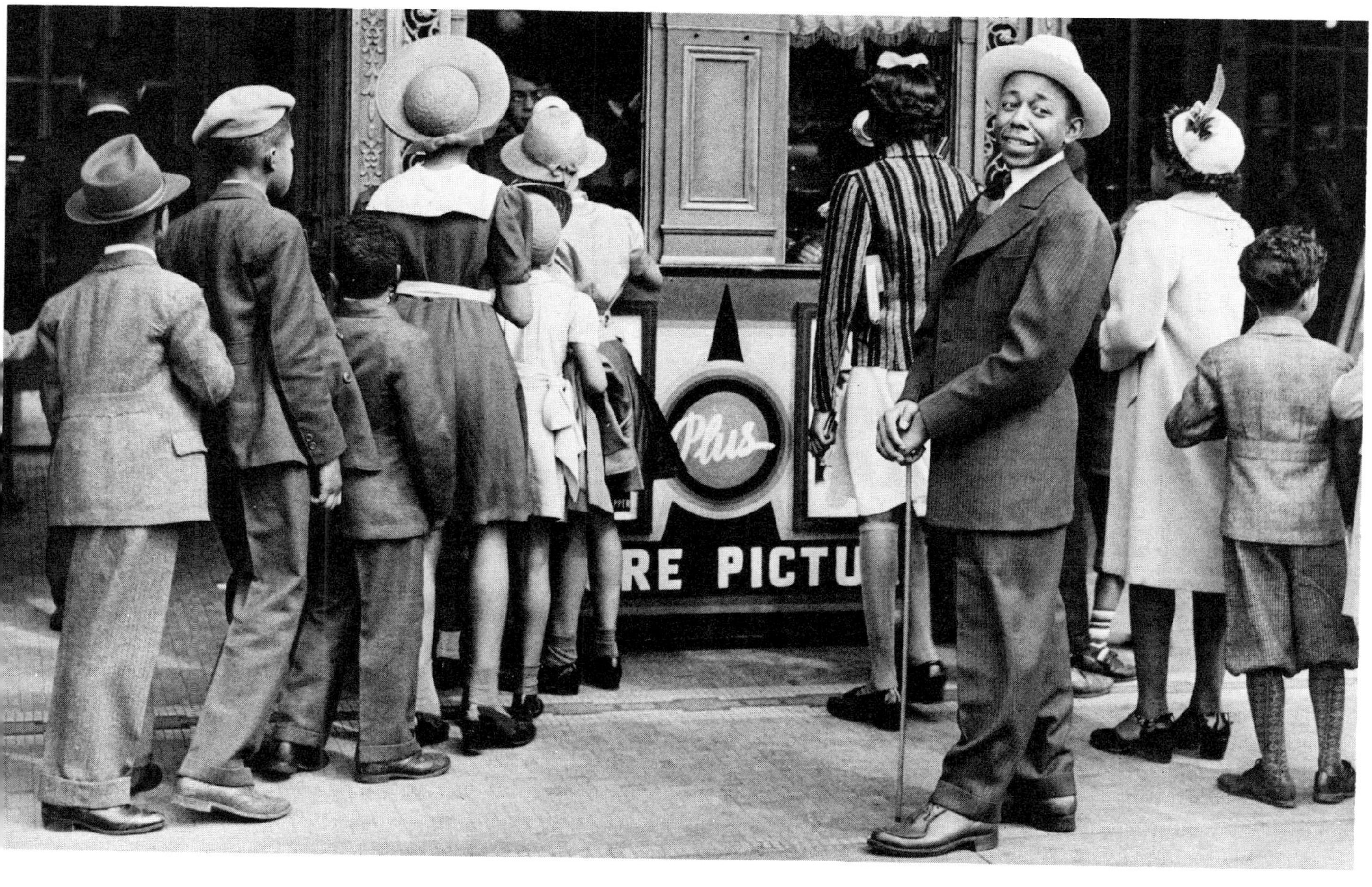
Plus

HOUND DOG TAYLOR
Photo by Dick Waterman
Courtesy of Alligator Records

Open G
Dropped C Tuning
(I)

RABBITS

Arvid Smith

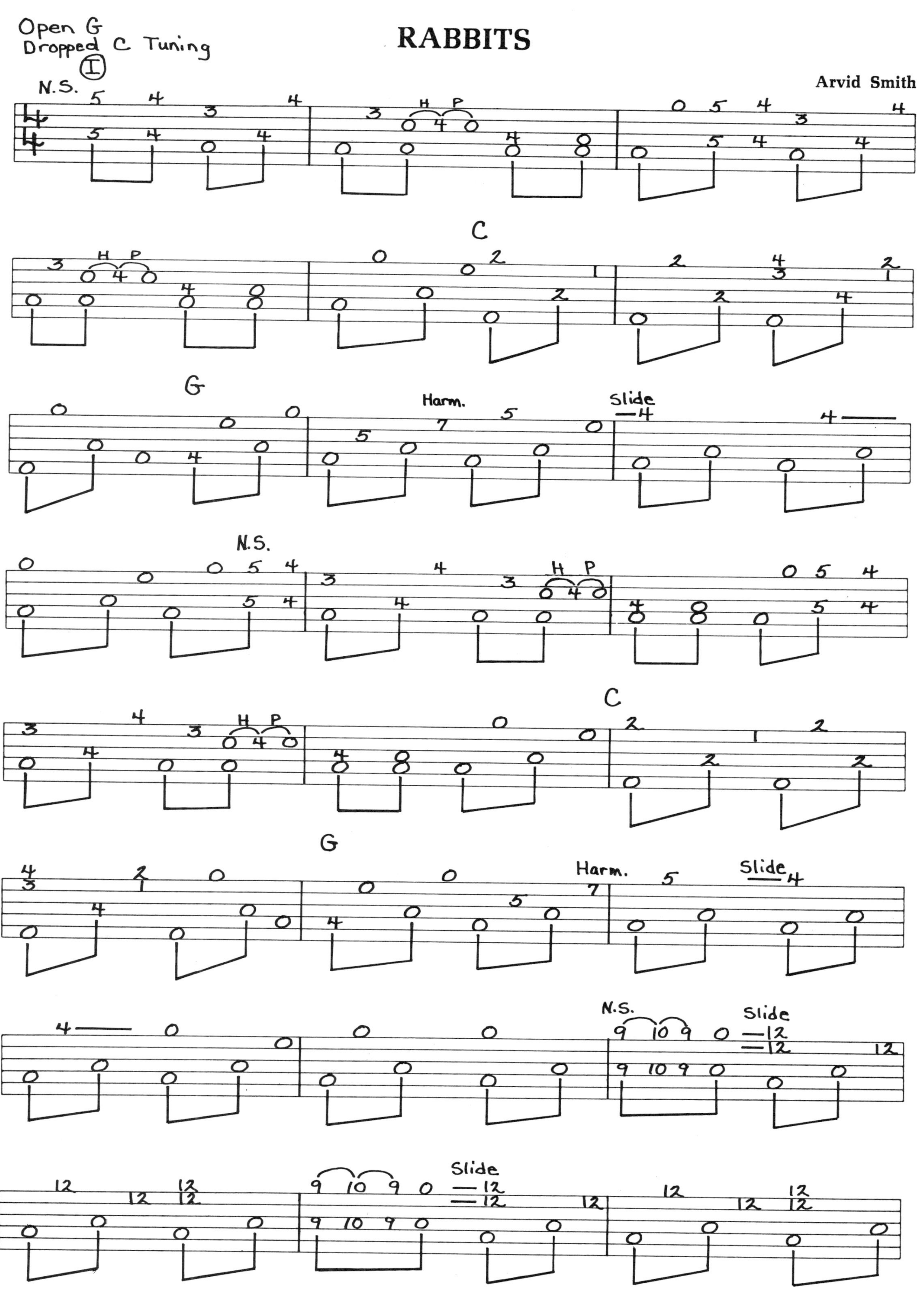

RABBITS

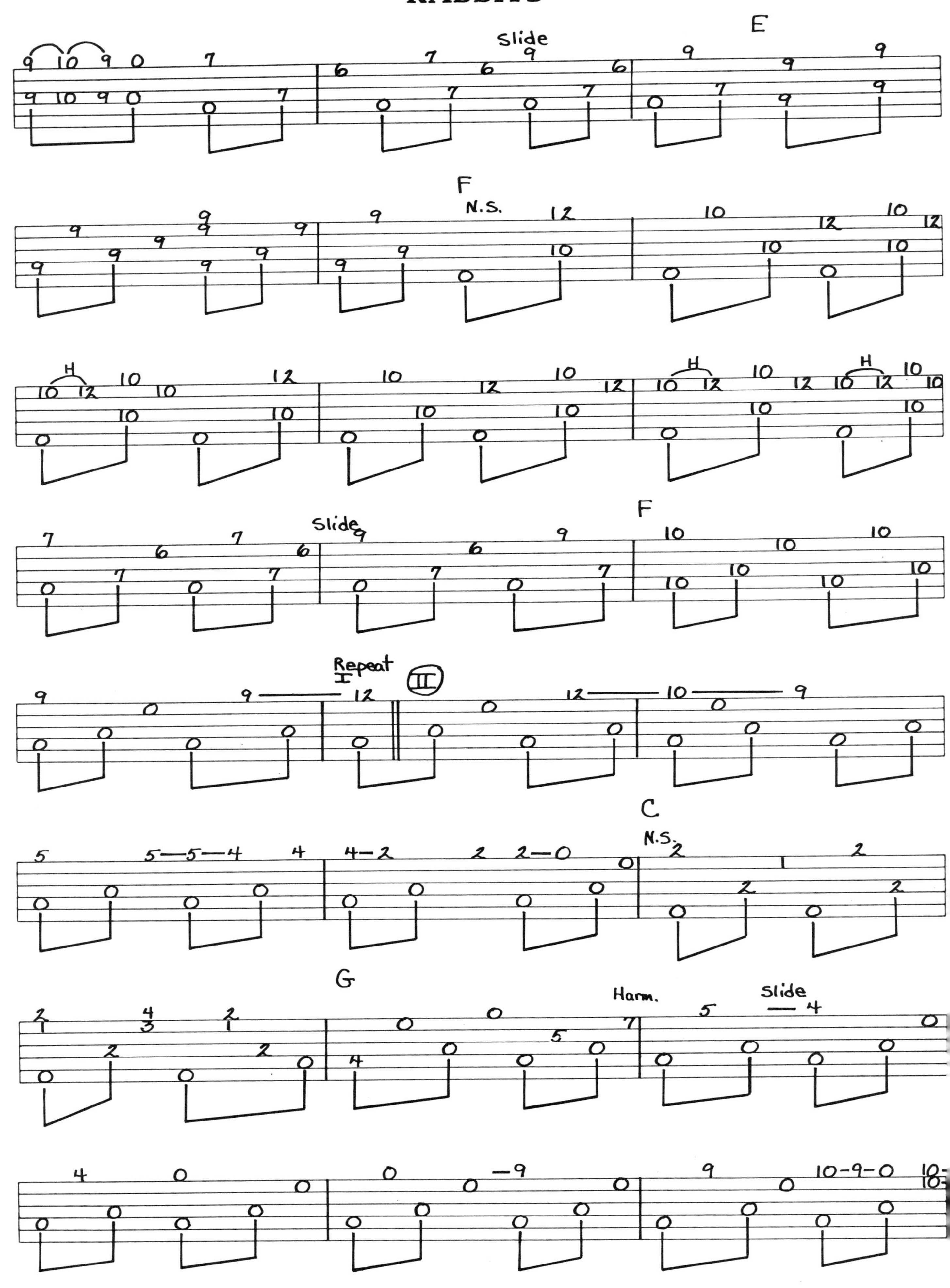

RABBITS

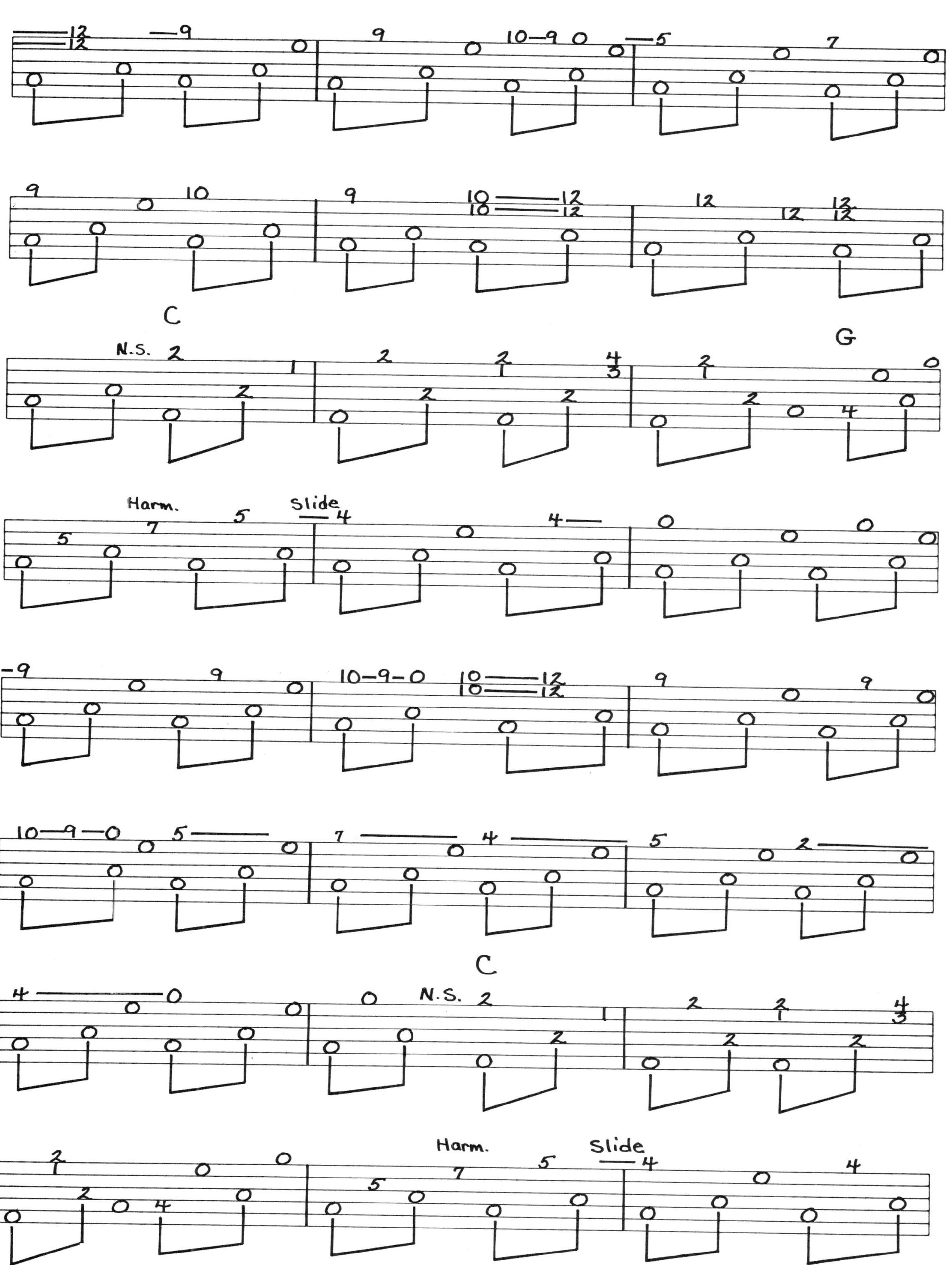

RABBITS

RABBITS

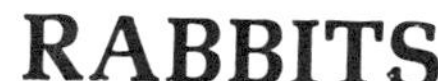

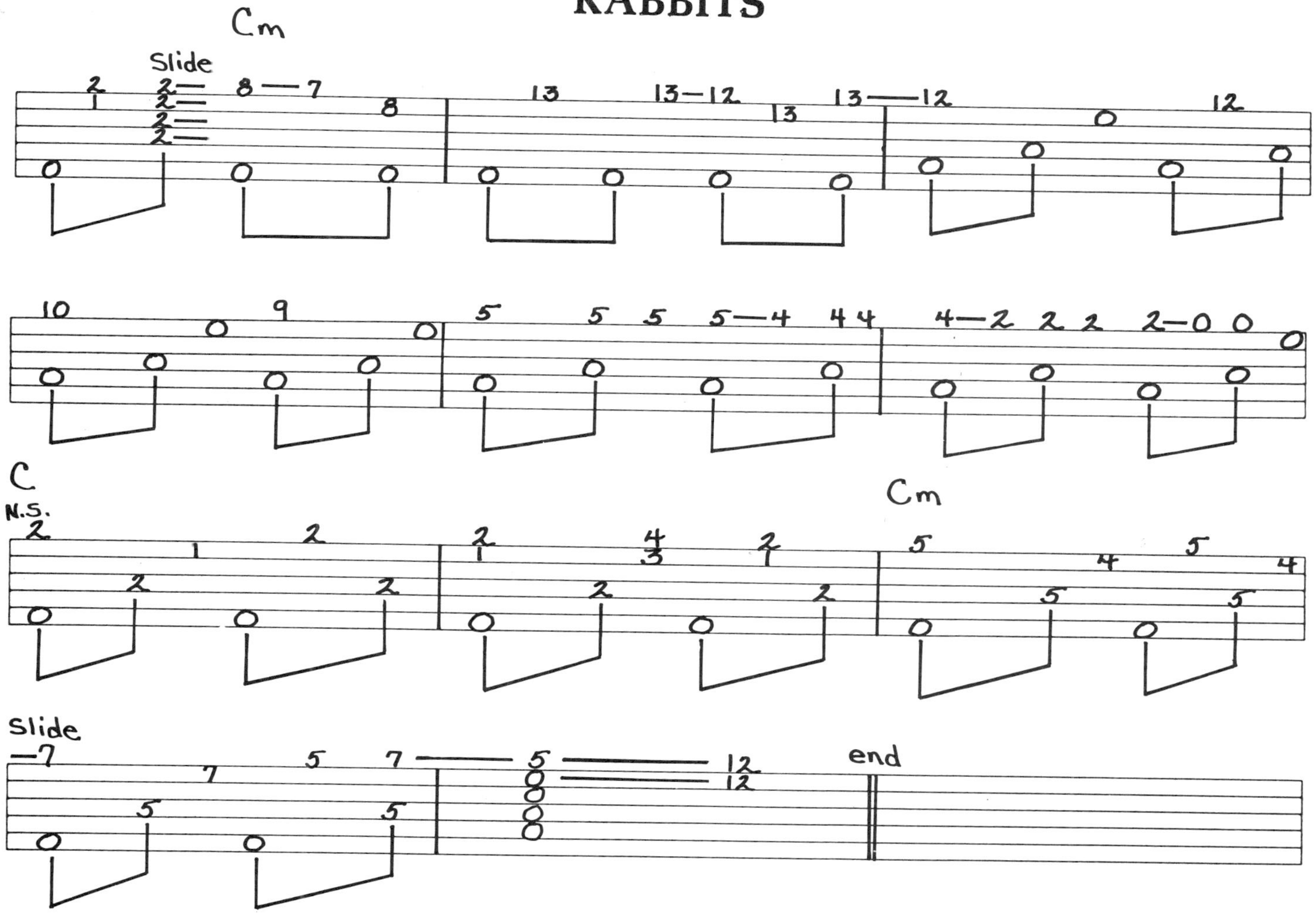
Cm
Slide
C
N.S.
Cm
Slide
end

I hope you enjoy this tuning as much as I have. If you get some good ideas about how to use it please drop us a line and lay 'em on us.

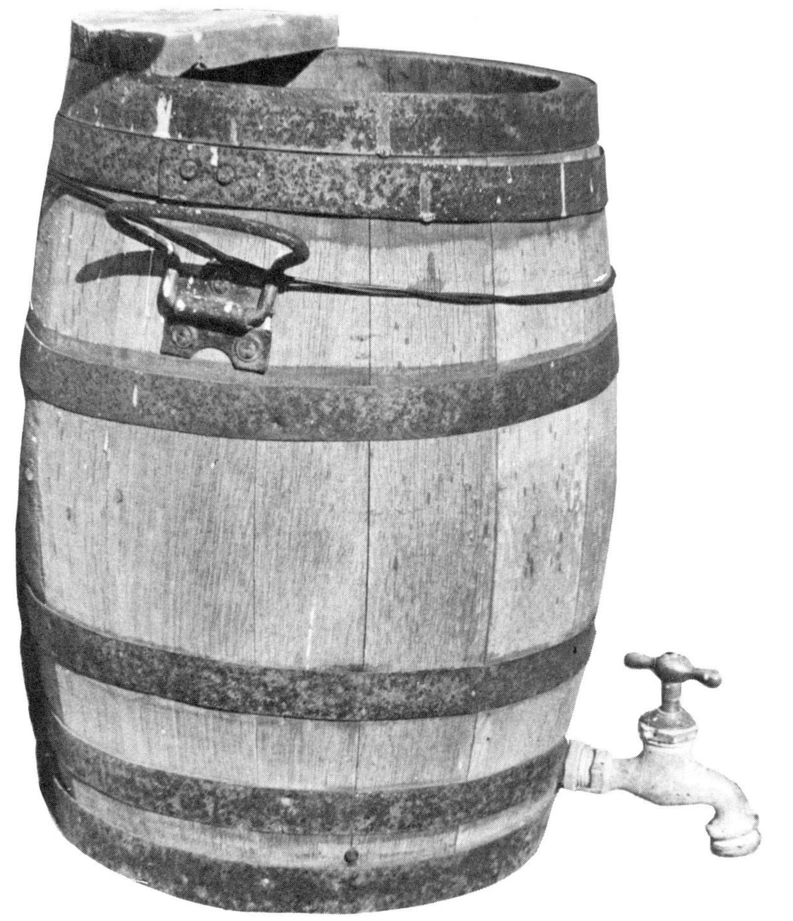

CHAPTER V
OPEN D TUNING

For the songs in this section the guitar is tuned into open D. From the standard tuning follow these steps.

1. Tune E6 string to one octave below D4 string.
2. Tune G3 string to 4th fret (F#) of D4 string.
3. Tune B2 string to 3rd fret (A) of 3rd (F#) string.
4. Tune E1 string to 5th fret (D) of 2nd (A) string.

Standard		Open D
E1	Lowered to	D
B	Lowered to	A
G	Lowered to	F#
D	Same	D
A	Same	A
E6	Lowered to	D

D tuning has a fine robust sound much like the E chord found in standard tuning. After G, it's probably the most common slide tuning. The high D on the 12th fret is great for a ringing tonic resolution and a lot can be done with extended slides on the upper strings.

OLD GEORGIA CAMPGROUNDS
Photo by Bob McClintock

PLAIN, WASH. CO., COLO., OCT. 1939
Photo by A. Rothstein
Library of Congress Collection

Photo by Alice Owen

Open D

POOR LAZARUS

Traditional
Arranged by Arvid Smith

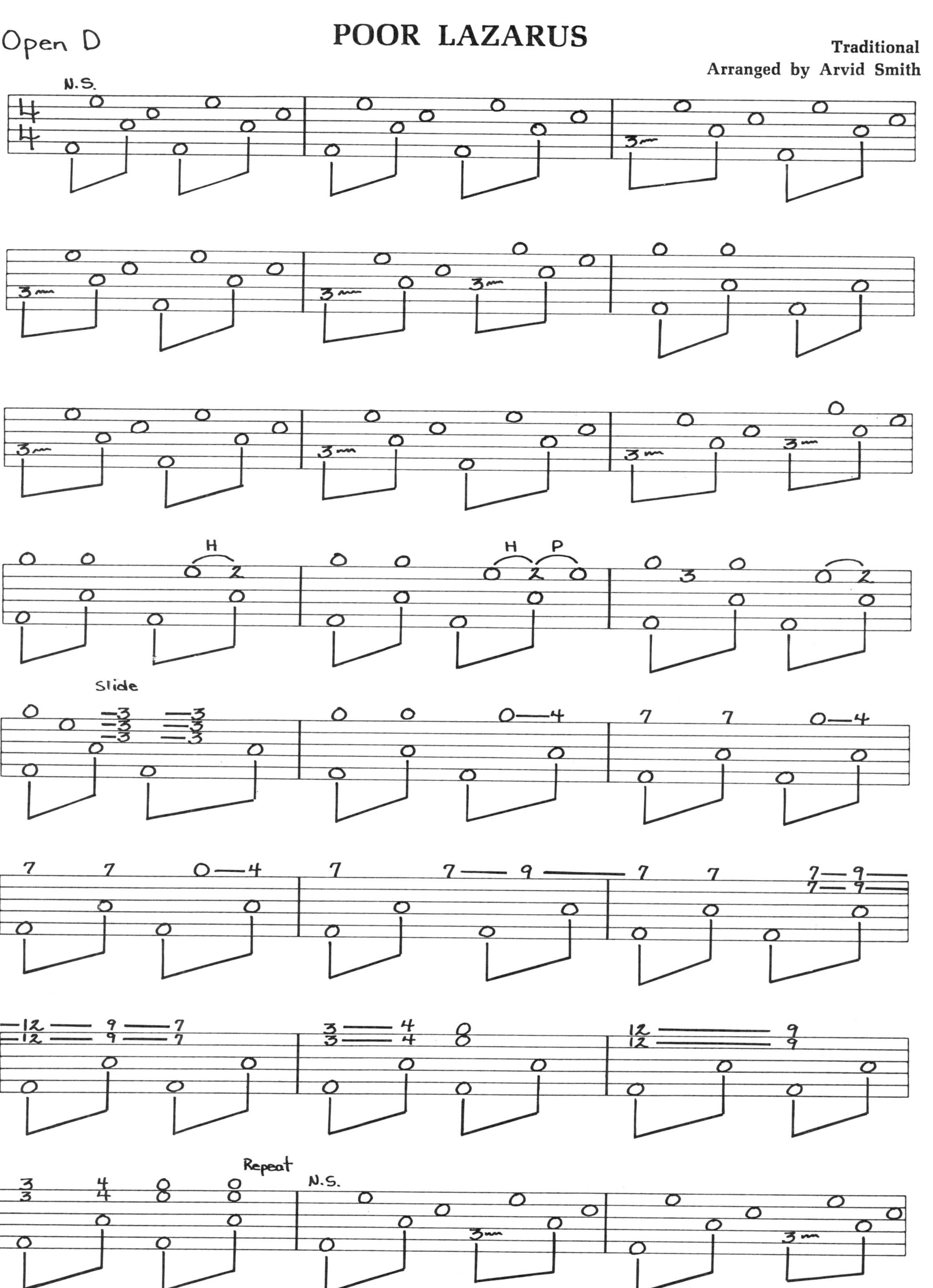

POOR LAZARUS

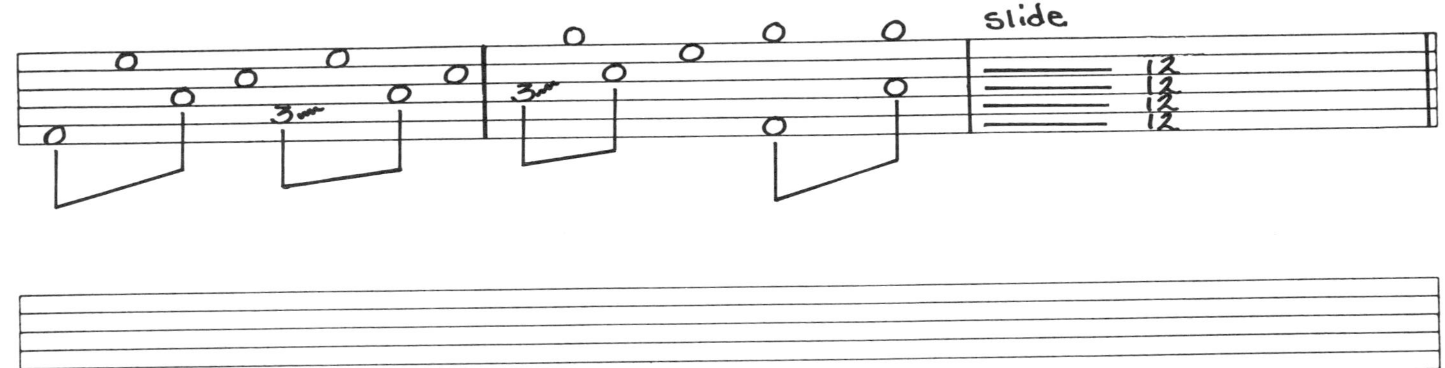

FUNERAL BIER, Photo by Bob McClintock

EVERYBODY OUGHT TO TREAT A STRANGER RIGHT

Traditional
Arranged by Arvid Smith

COTTON SHARECROPPERS-GEORGIA 1937
Photo by D. Lange
Library of Congress Collection

EZRA FOX

Arvid Smith

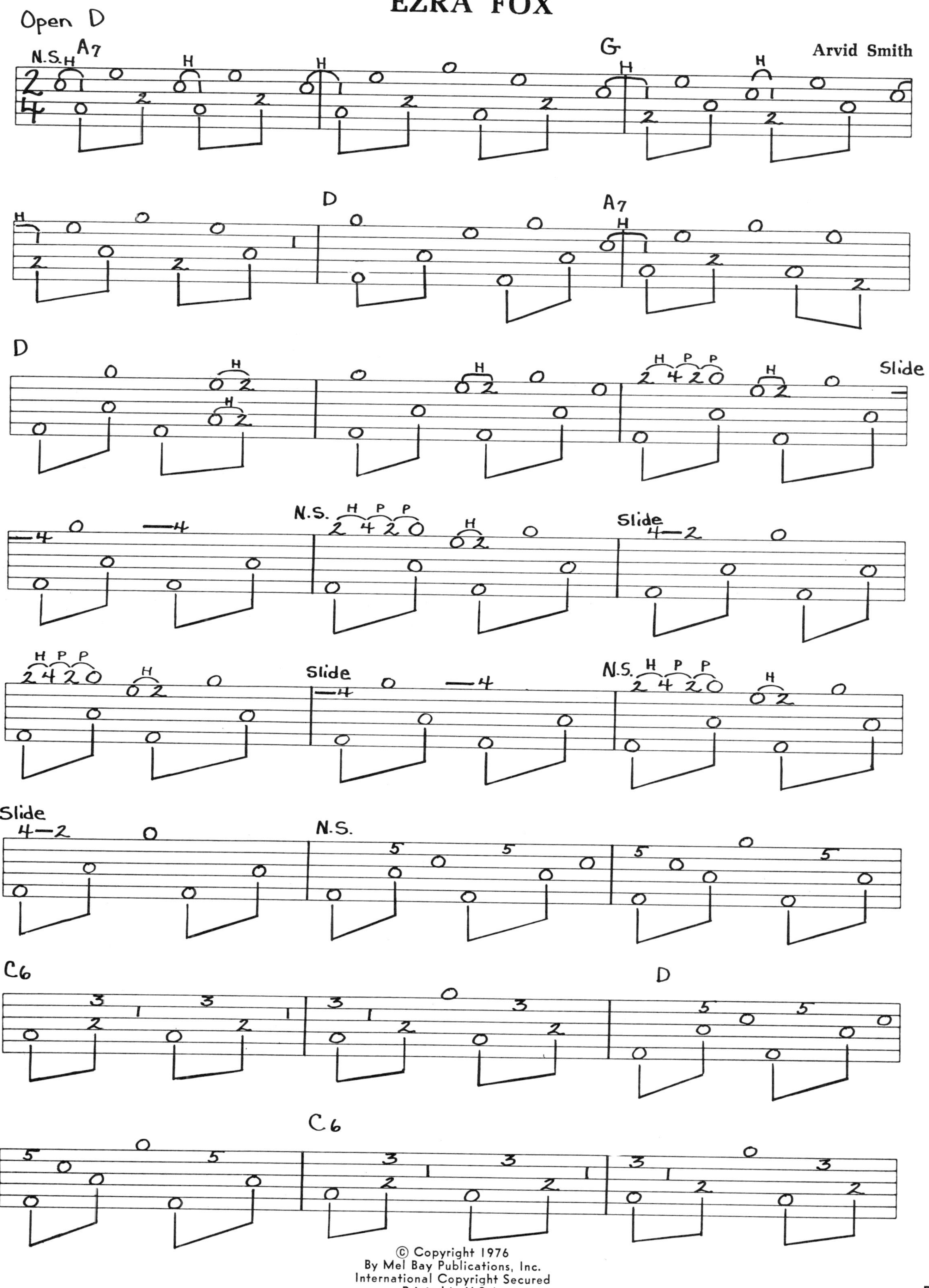

EZRA FOX

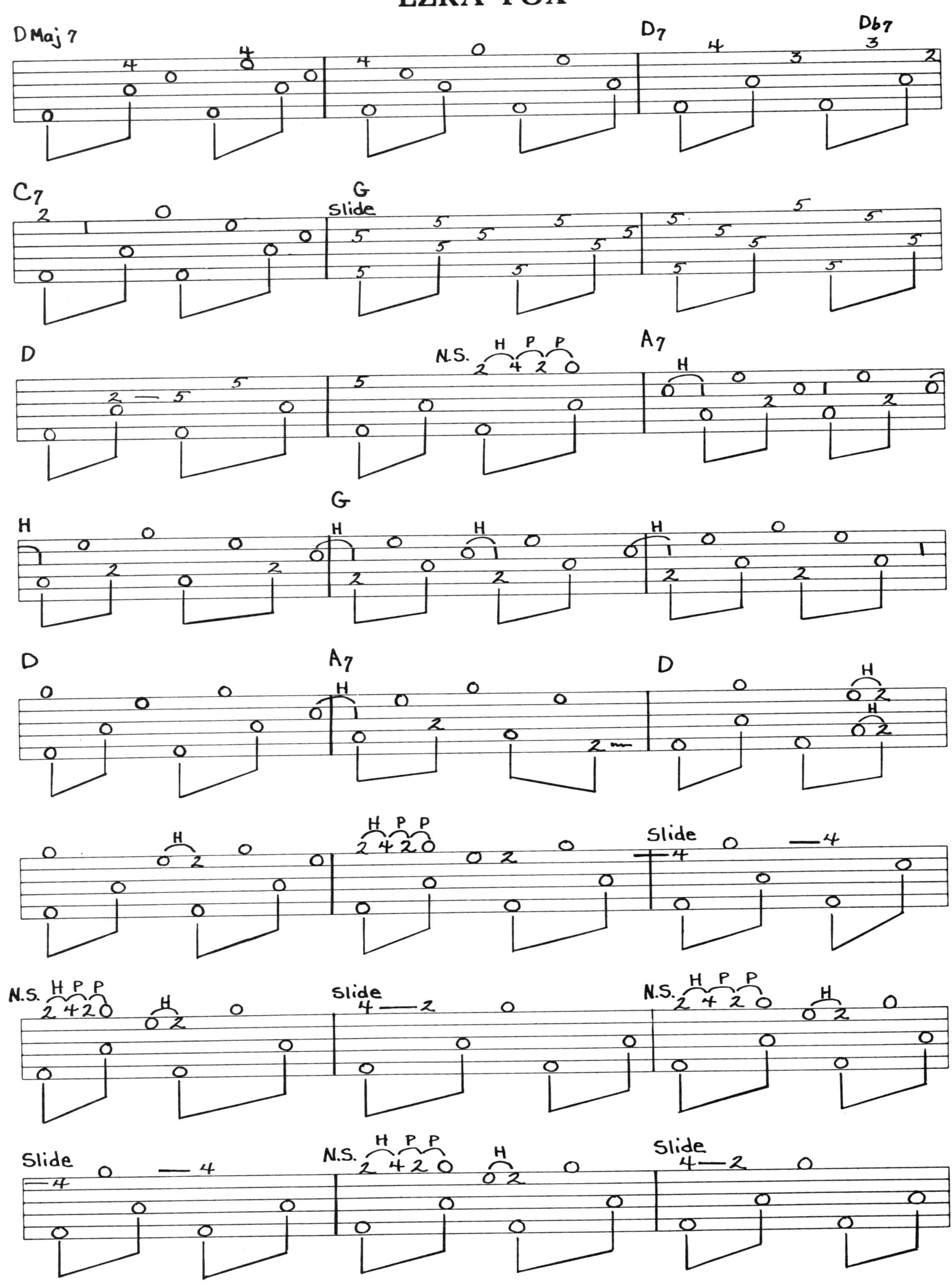

DMaj 7
D7
Db7
C7
G
Slide
D
N.S.
H P P
A7
H
G
D
A7
D
Slide
N.S.
Slide
N.S.
Slide
N.S.
Slide

EZRA FOX

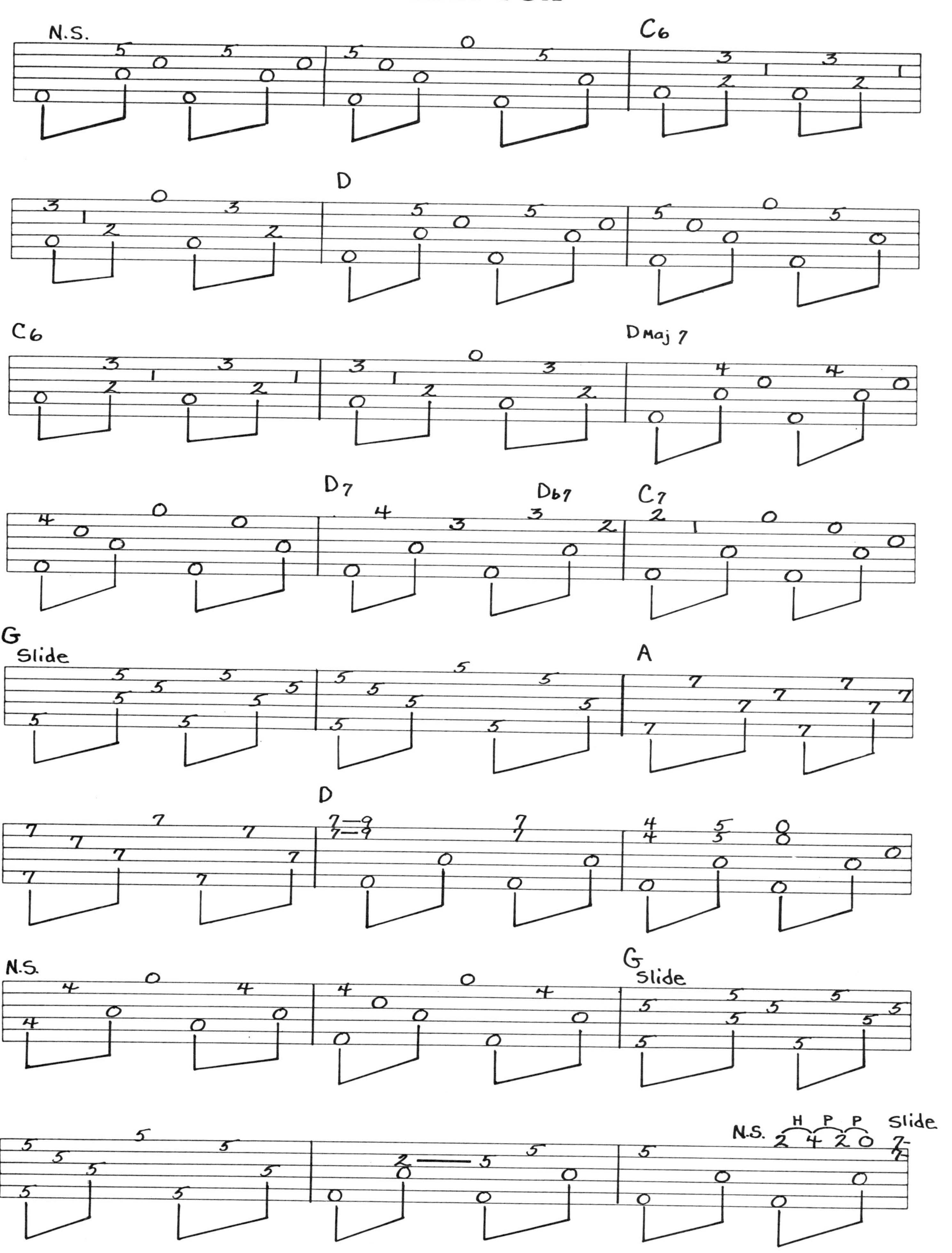

EZRA FOX

EZRA FOX

Library of Congress Collection

Listen to **My Black Mama** by Son House or **Poor Boy** by John Fahey for two demonstrations of how D tuning can be used. Several good musicians use this tuning raised to E. Blind Willie Johnson's **Dark Was the Night, Cold Was the Ground** is a good example of E tuning and its possibilities.

CHAPTER VI
OPEN D6 TUNING

Open D6 tuning gives an interesting sound. When I learned **Whistling Blues** by Reverend Gary Davis, I liked the tuning so much I composed a couple of songs in it.

To get to open D6 tuning first place the guitar in open D tuning. Then all you have to do is place a finger on the second fret of the second string and lower the first string to match that note.

Open D		Open D6
D	Lowered to	B
A	Same	A
F#	Same	F#
D	Same	D
A	Same	A
D	Same	D

Here's a song designed for a bit of comic relief. The sound of the D6 tuning gives the effect of an old player piano or music box tune. All notes are sounded with the slide. The song is played at an even walking tempo and at end the tempo slows down while your slide slowly eases down the neck toward the first fret constantly dropping the pitches. This is indicated by the X's and gives the sound of an old victrola giving out. I did not play the ending this way on the instruction record. But if you choose to do so just follow the tablature and be the life of the party. Have fun.

Library of Congress Collection

ERODED LAND IN NORTH CAROLINA 1938
Photo by Post-Wolcott
Library of Congress Collection

MY MASTER'S VOICE

Arvid Smith

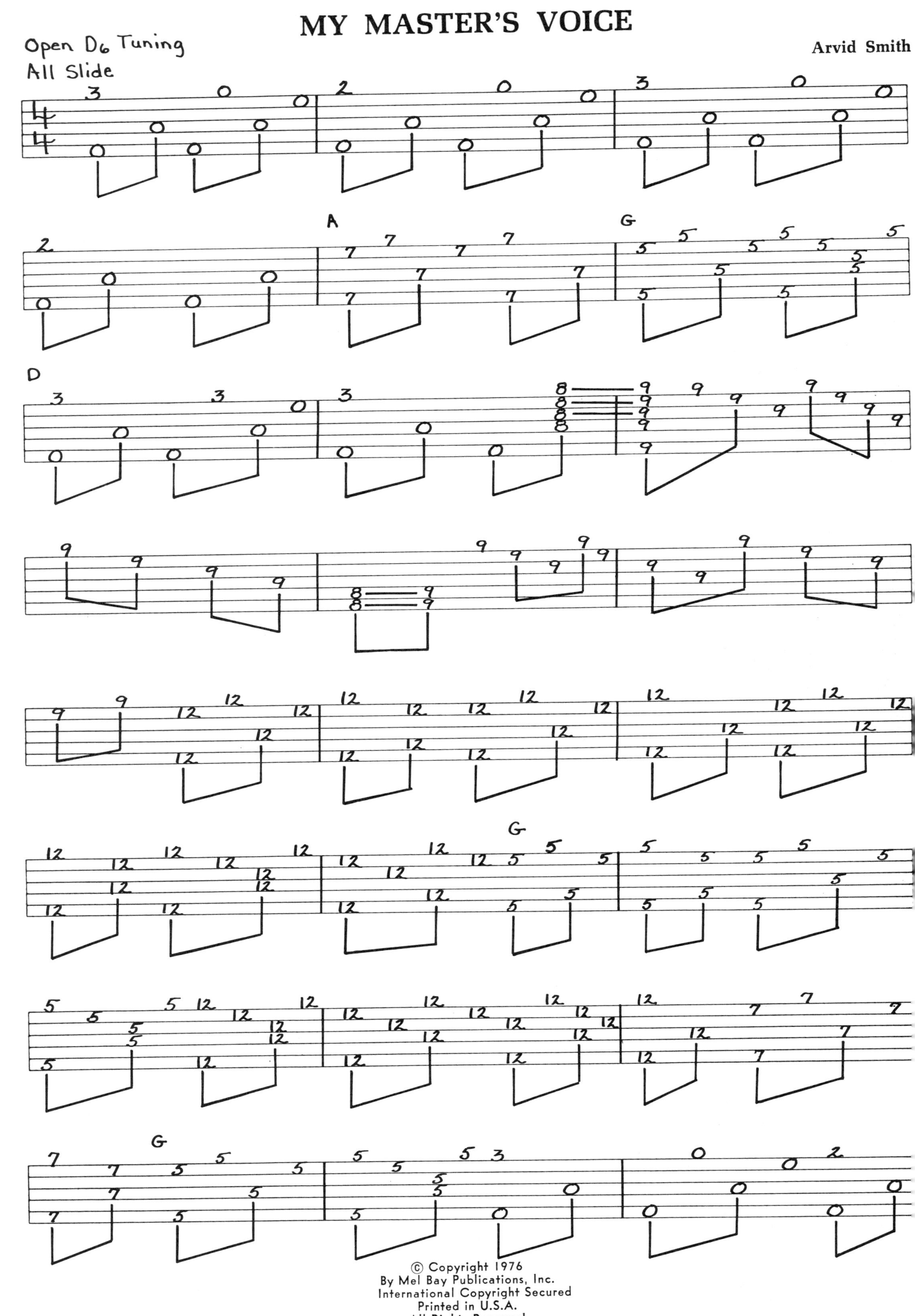

MY MASTER'S VOICE

Photo by Library of Congress Collection

Photo by Bob McClintock

Open D6

CARNIVAL IN COSTA RICA

Arvid Smith

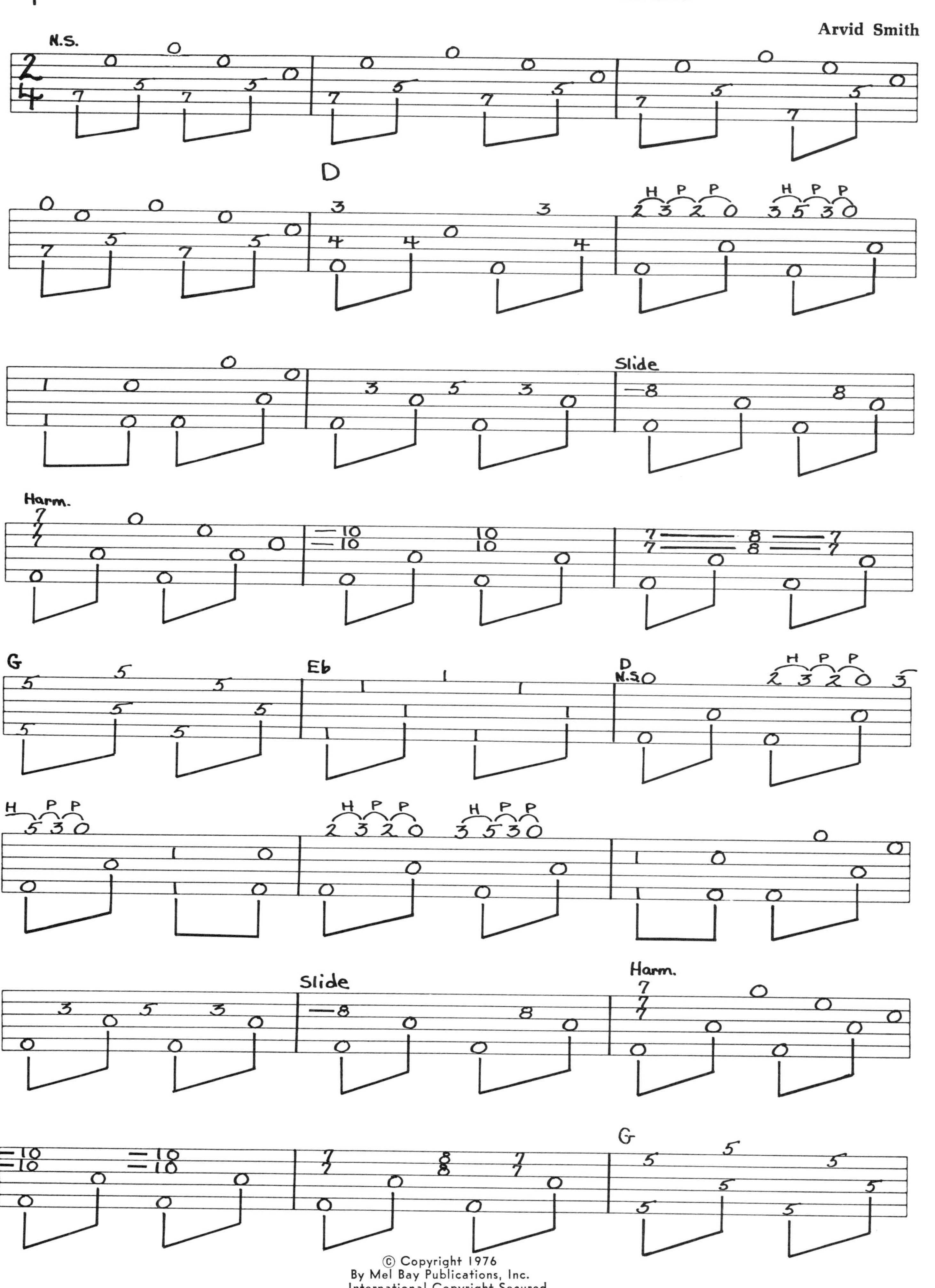

CARNIVAL IN COSTA RICA

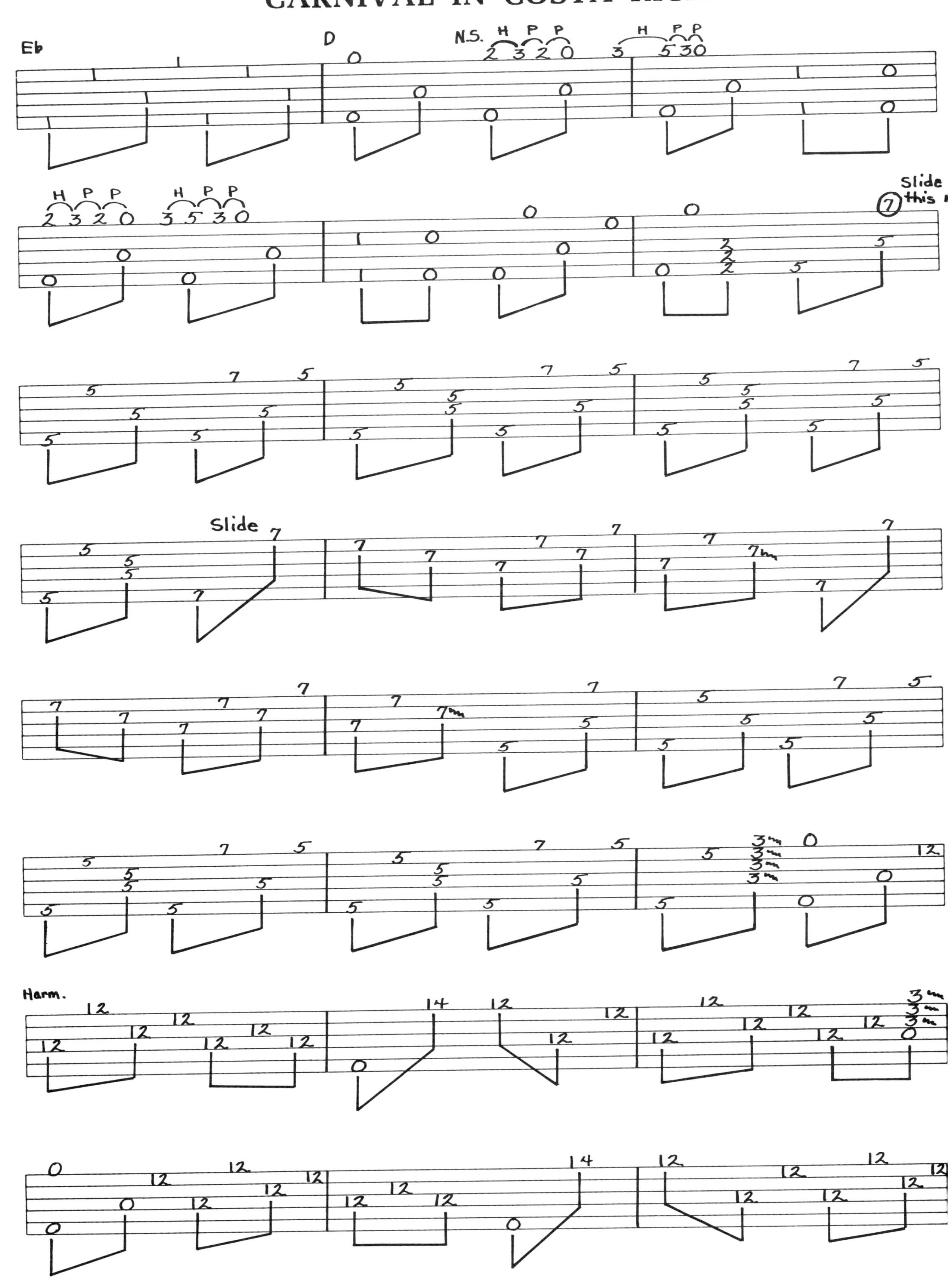

CARNIVAL IN COSTA RICA

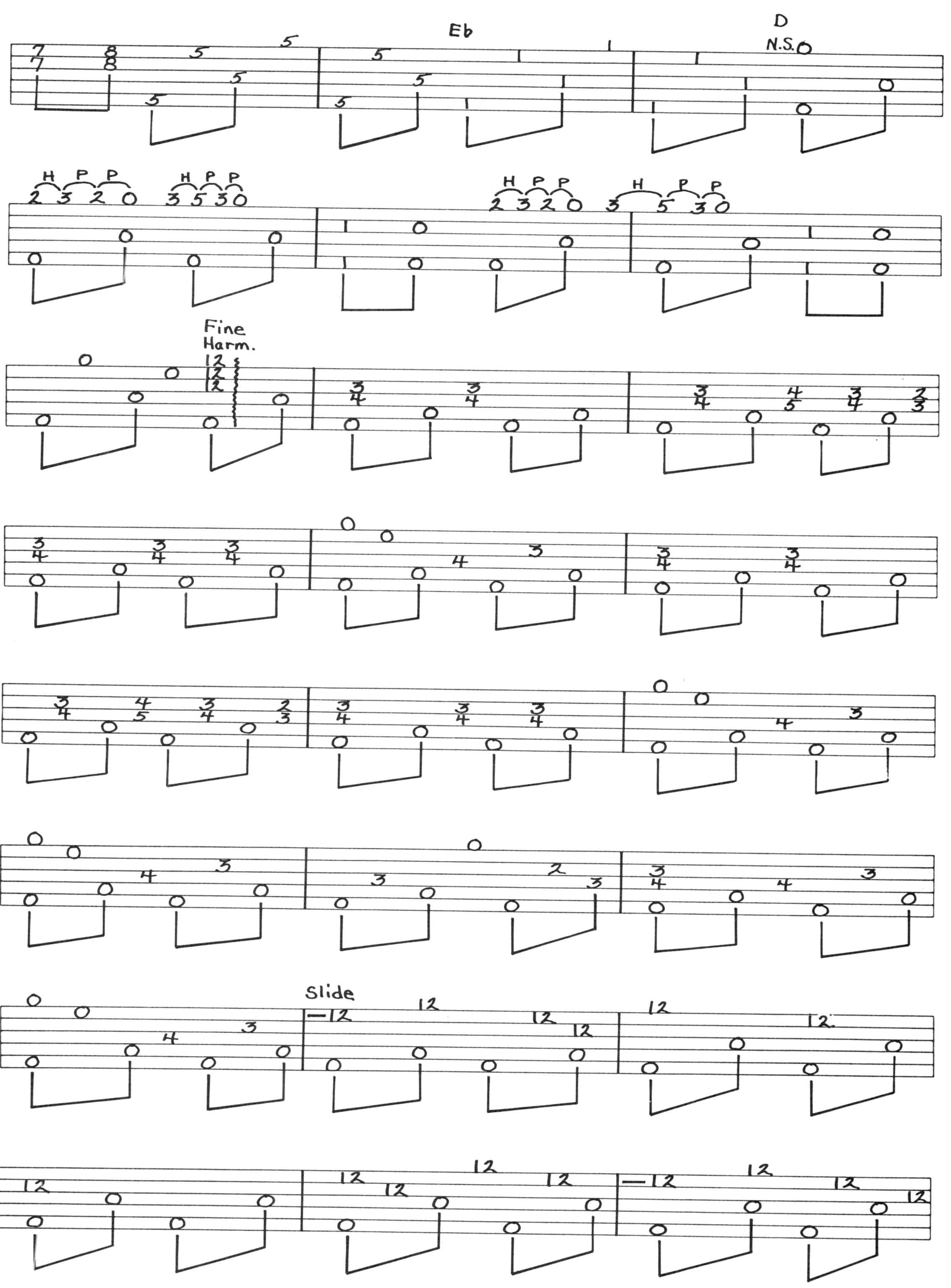

CARNIVAL IN COSTA RICA

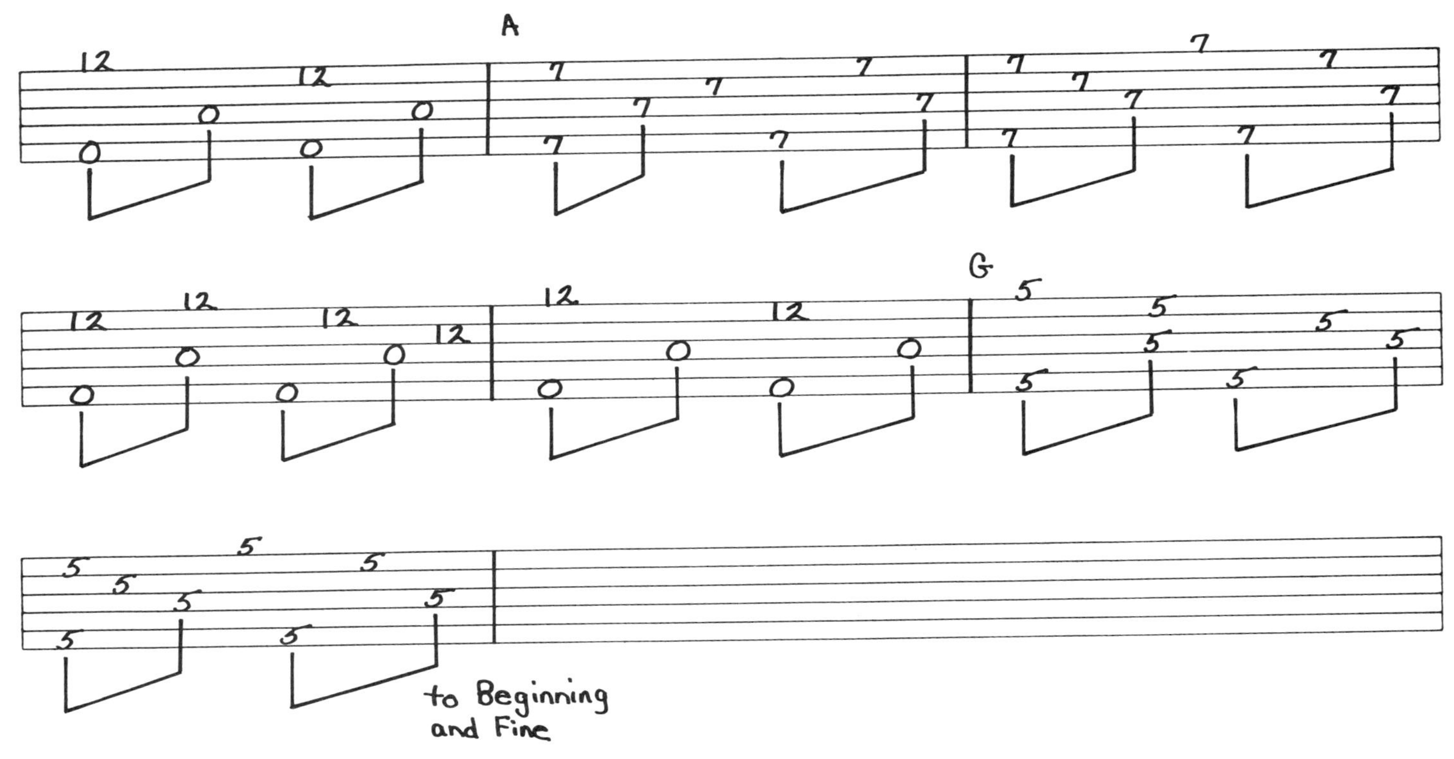

Use D6 tuning like chili pepper—a little goes a long way.

Photo by Bob McClintock

CHAPTER VII
OPEN C TUNING

This is another tuning commonly used for slide guitar. In this tuning the strings are altered to a much greater degree than in the other tunings. To get to open C from standard tuning:

1. Place the finger on the fifth fret of the third string (G) and raise the second string (B) to match that note.
2. Tune the fourth string (D) to one octave below the second (now C) string.
3. Tune the sixth string (E6) to one octave below the fourth (now C) string.
4. Tune the fifth string (A) to one octave below the third string (G).

Standard		Open C
E1	Same	E
B	Raised to	C
G	Same	G
D	Lowered to	C
A	Lowered to	G
E6	Lowered to	C

WADE IN THE WATER

Traditional Spiritual
Arranged by Arvid Smith

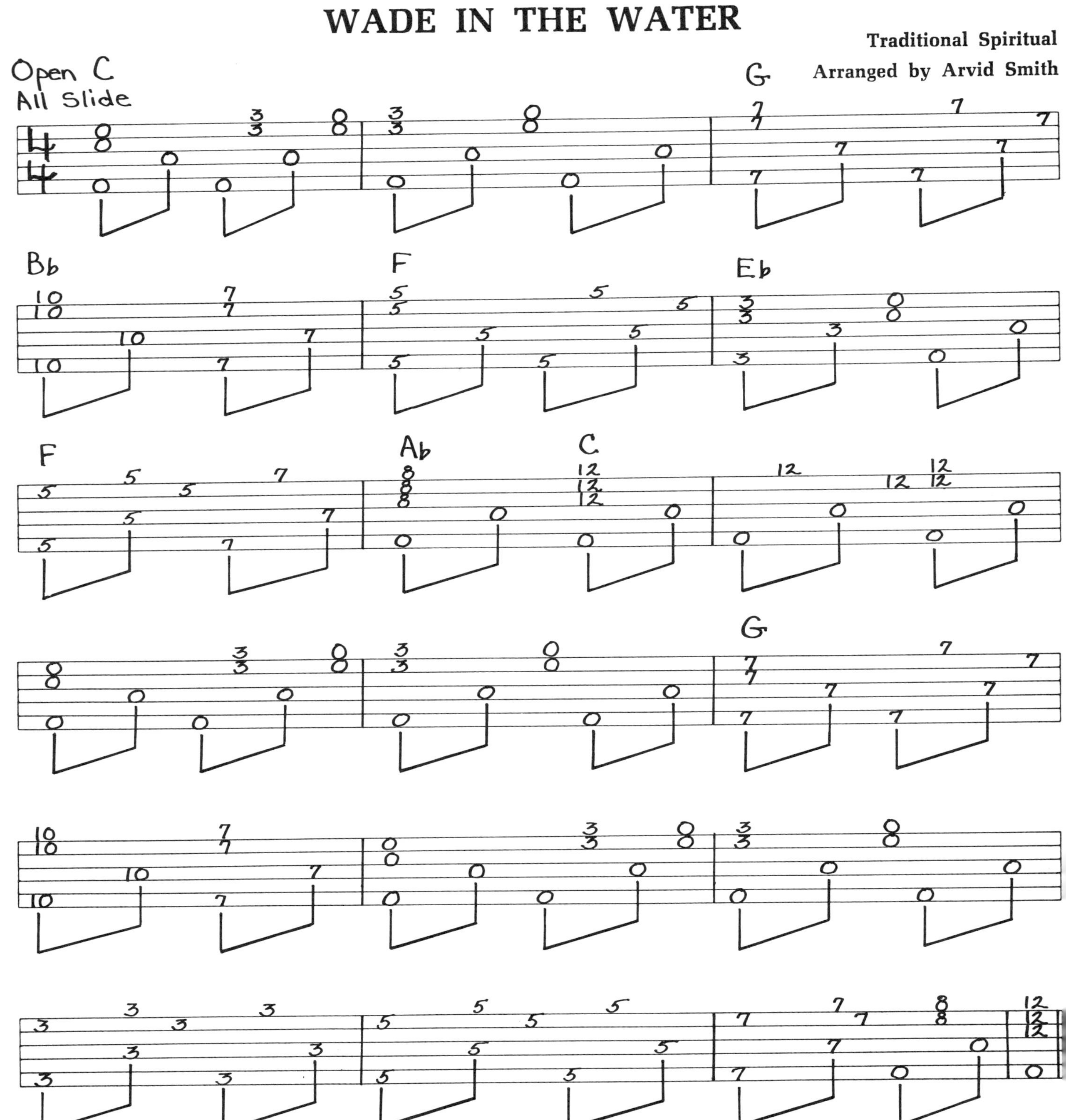

GRANDCHILDREN FROLICKING
Photo by Barbara McClintock Koehler

WHITE WATER, Photo by Bob McClintock

Open C tuning, like D6, is a good variety tuning. The lack of a tonic or dominant note on the top string limits its usefulness for blues, but opens up new opportunities in other directions. Leo Kottke's **Watermelon** and **Busted Bicycle** are in open C as are Peter Lang's **Wide Oval Ripoff** and John Fahey's **Funeral Song For Mississippi John Hurt.** Again, if you come up with new and different ways to use open C let us know about them.

I'm available. If you have problems, questions, or comments you can write to me at Sunny Mountain Records.

If you devise a new tuning or if you develop a new slant on slide playing, please let me be the first to know.

Arvid Smith

LOOSE ENDS

The purpose of this book has been to demonstrate the uses of slide guitar styles in solo fingerpicked guitar pieces. As you all out there know, the guitar is at home in most any musical style so likewise the slide technique can also find its own place in any player's house of music.

For all you solo singer-songwriters wishing to add a little extra spice to your arrangements, try playing your chords in an open tuning with a slide. Not all songs will sound just great with bottleneck (for heaven's sake don't do it with **Greensleeves)** but you never can tell what new ideas you can come up with once you're in an open tuning. You'll also find that instrumental breaks are a whole lot easier with these tunings. Examples of what an open tuning and a little slide can do for your basic folk song can be heard on any Ry Cooder album.

The slide can also be used to get a sitar-like quality out of single string melodies. An example that comes to mind is the introduction to John Fahey's **On the Banks of the Owchita** on his Takoma Vol. III (see discography). Here the guitar is in open C tuning with an ascending-descending melody line played with a slide—that as the notes drop down a zingy vibrato is used to sustain the notes—which produces a very Indian type sound.

Another way to get different sounds is by using what are called "unsion" tunings. As the name implies, in these tunings two adjacent strings are tuned to the same note. Check out the John Fahey "Requia" album and his Takoma Vol. IV for the uses of his open C unison (strings tuned from 6 to 1: C G C G **C C.** For his bottleneck song **I Am the Resurrection** on the Takoma Vol. V he uses a

(continued next page)

G unison tuning (D G D **G G** D). Another fine example is the bottleneck accompaniment to the song **Chevrolet** by the Jim Kweskin Jug Band (Vanguard 79234). On this tune a D unison (D A **D D** A D) is used.

Some more unusual tunings not discussed in this book are the various "modal" tunings. In these tunings the third of the chord is tuned to the fourth. I think this is also called "sawmill" tuning among banjo pickers but that's another book. A couple of examples are G modal (D G D G **C** D) and D modal (D A D **G** A D).

One area which was not touched on at all was lap style playing. This was not the purpose of this book as we also used our fingers as well as the slide to fret the notes. There are plenty of fine instruction books in Dobro®, Hawaiian steel and full pedal steel guitar available today but that doesn't stop me from throwing in at least one tip. For all my Hawaiian brothers out there who are tired of the same old E7 tuning (B D E G# B E) I have a slight variation which you may or may not know about. I call it the E7/E6 tuning and it goes like this: B D E G# B **C#**. I have an ancient six string lap steel that I fool around with and I was surprised at the different chord qualities I could get with this tuning without slanting the bar. If you're up on your music theory like I was at the time you'll find out that majors, minors, sevenths, minor sevenths, and sixths are readily available.

With all this talk of different tunings let us not leave out the one with which we all grew up. By this I mean good old standard tuning (E A D G B E). To some this is the only real tuning but that too is another book. The uses for slide in standard tuning are as evident as in the others. One of the commonly used bar chord positions is the **A major** type chord barred up the neck. By using just the back three notes of this chord (the ones on the second, third and fourth strings) and fretting those notes with the slide, major chords become a snap to play. The first four strings of a barred **E minor** type chord are a natural for the minor also. For slide leadwork in standard tuning a great example is the playing of Rory Gallagher, the Irish Wonder, particularly on the "Irish Tour" (see discography) LP.

This book was designed to give you a new slant on guitar playing as well as instructing you to the nature of slide guitar playing. Remember, above all, to let the musician in you use these particular slide voicings to their proper degree. In other words learn when **not** to use them.

Photo by Bill Koehler

APPENDIX I
DISCOGRAPHY

ADELPHI 10075 - Furry Lewis, Bukka White, Gus Cannon "On The Road Again"

ADVENT 2803 - Johnnie Shines

ALLIGATOR 4701 - Hound Dog Taylor and the House-rockers
4704 - Hound Dog Taylor and The House-rockers "Natural Boogie"

ARCHIVE OF FOLK FS 253 - Mississippi Fred McDowell

ARHOOLIE F 1001 - "Mance Lipscomb - Texas Share-cropper and Songster"
F 1003 - "Black Ace"
F 1005 - "I Have To Paint My Face (Various Artists)
F 1006 - "Blues N' Trouble" (Various Artists)
F 1017 - "Texas Blues - Vol. 2" (Various Artists)
F 1018 - "Bad Luck N' Trouble" (Various Artists)
F 1019 - Bukka White "Sky Songs - Vol. 1"
F 1020 - Bukka White "Sky Songs - Vol. 2"
F 1021 - Fred McDowell "Mississippi Delta Blues"
F 1027 - Fred McDowell "Vol. 2"
1041 - "Mississippi Delta Blues - Vol. 1" (Various Artists)
1046 - Fred McDowell "& His Blue Boys"
1055 - Johnnie Lewis "Alabama Slide Guitar"

ARHOOLIE 1068 - Fred McDowell "Keep Your Light Trimmed and Burning"
R 2001/2002 - "The Roots Of America's Music" (Various Artists)

ATCO SD 7004 - Rory Gallagher "Deuce"

ATLANTIC RSO or QD 4801 - Eric Clapton "461 Ocean Boulevard"
SD 1348 - "Roots Of The Blues" (Fred McDowell cuts)
SD 7224 - Blind Willie McTell "Blues Originals - Vol. 1"

BIOGRAPH BLP 12008 - Blind Willie McTell (1949)
BLP 12017 - Fred McDowell, Furry Lewis
BLP 12035 - Blind Willie McTell, Memphis Minnie
BLP 12040 - Son House, Blind Lemon Jefferson
BLP 12044 - Johnnie Shines
BLP 12048 - Johnnie Shines and Co.
BLP 12049 - Bukka White "Big Daddy"

BLUE GOOSE 2002 - Graham Hine "Bottleneck Blues"
2003 - "These Blues Is Meant To Be Barrelhoused" (Various Artists)

BLUE HORIZON 4610 - Johnnie Shines

BLUES CLASSICS BC 4 - Peetie Wheatstraw and Kokomo Arnold
BC 6 - "Country Blues Classics - Vol. 2" (Various Artists)

BLUES CLASSICS BC 8 - "Chicago Blues - The Early 50's (Various Artists)
BC 11 - Blind Boy Fuller
BC 15 - "Memphis and The Delta - The 1950's" (Various Artists)
BC 25 - Tampa Red

CAPITOL ST 409 - Mississippi Fred McDowell "I Do Not Play No Rock N' Roll"
ST 682 - Leo Kottke "Mudlark"
ST 11000 - Leo Kottke "Greenhouse"
ST 11164 - Leo Kottke "My Feet Are Smiling"
ST 11262 - Leo Kottke "Ice Water"
ST 11335 - Leo Kottke "Dreams & All That Stuff"

CAPRICORN 2CP 0102 - Allman Brothers "Eat A Peach"
2CP 0108 - "Duane Allman - An Anthology"
2CX 0131 - Allman Brothers "Live At The Filmore East"
2CX 0132 - Allman Brothers "Beginnings"
CPO 0136 - Johnny Jenkins "Ton Ton Macoute"
2CP 0139 - "Duane Allman Anthology - Vol. II"
0150 - Grinderswitch "Macon Tracks"

CHESS LP 1537 - Elmore James/John Brim "Whose Muddy Shoes"

CHESS CH 50033 - Muddy Waters "Fathers and Sons"

CHESS 2CH 60006 - "McKinley Morganfield A.K.A. Muddy Waters"

COLUMBIA GP 18 - Taj Mahal "Giant Step - De Old Folks At Home"

COLUMBIA CL 1654 - Robert Johnson "King Of The Delta Blues Singers"
CS 9579 - Taj Mahal
CS 9826 - Johnny Winter
KSC 9947 - Johnny Winter "Second Winter"
G 30008 - Bukka White, Robert Johnson, Elmore James, Johnny Shines, Willie McTell, etc. "The Story Of The Blues"
C 30034 - Robert Johnson "King Of The Delta Blues Singers" (Different selection from CL 1654)
CQ or KC 32188 - Johnny Winter "Still Alive & Well"

DELMARK DS 617 - J. B. Hutto and The Hawks "Hawk Squat"
DS 636 - J. B. Hutto and The Hawks "Slide Winder"

FLYRIGHT LP 101 - "Kings Of The Twelve String" (Various Artists)

FOLKLYRIC 9002 - Son House

FOLKWAYS RF 10 - Blind Willie Johnson (1927 - 1930)
RF 11 - "Blues Rediscoveries" (Various Artists)
RF 14 - "Blues Roots/Mississippi" (Various Artists)
RF 15 - "The Atlanta Blues" (Various Artists)
RF 202 - "The Rural Blues" (Various Artists)
2467 - Son House/J. D. Short
3585 - "Blind Willie Johnson Blues"

HERWIN 201 - "Sic Em Dogs One Me" (1927 - 1939; Various Artists)

HISTORICAL HLP 31 - "Masters Of The Blues" (1928 - 1940; Various Artists)

KENT KST 522 - Elmore James "Original Folk Blues"
KST 9001 - Elmore James "Anthology Of The Blues"
KST 9010 - "Anthology Of The Blues - Resurrection of Elmore James"

KICKING MULE 109 - Stefan Grossman and Aurora Block "How To Play Blues Guitar"

LIBERTY LBS 83391 - Son House "John The Revelator (English import)

LONDON NPS 4 - Rolling Stones "Let It Bleed"

MCA MCA 363 - Lynyrd Skynyrd "Pronounced Leh-Nerd Skin-Nerd"
MCA 413 - Lynyrd Skynyrd "Second Helping"

MELODEON MLP 7323 - Blind Willie McTell (1940)

MILESTONE 3003 - Mississippi Fred McDowell "Long Way From Home"

MUSCADINE 1 - "On The Road Again" (Various Artists)

OLD TIMEY X 113 - " Steel Guitar Classics"

ORIGIN JAZZ LIBRARY OJL 1 - Charlie Patton
OJL 2 - "Really The Country Blues" (Various Artists)
OJL 5 - "Mississippi Blues - Vol. 1" (Various Artists)
OJL 7 - "Charlie Patton - Vol. 2"
OJL 11 - "Mississippi Blues - Vol. 2" (Various Artists)
OJL 13 - "In The Spirit - Vol. 2" (Various Artists)
OJL 17 - "Mississippi Blues - Vol. 3" (Various Artists)

PARAMOUNT (JUST SUNSHINE JSS 4 - Mississippi Fred McDowell

PARROTT 71036 - Savoy Brown "Raw Sienna"
71047 - Savoy Brown "Street Corner Talking"

POLYDOR 25-3002 - John Mayall "Back To The Roots"
2-3501 - Eric Clapton "Layla"
5513 - Rory Gallagher "Live"
5522 - Rory Gallagher "Blueprint"
5539 - Rory Gallagher "Tattoo"
2-9501 - Rory Gallagher "Irish Tour 74"

POLYDOR-INTERNATIONAL 423249 - Fred McDowell "Cotton Country Blues"

PRESTIGE 7388 - Homesick James "Blues On The South Side"
7809 - Blind Willie McTell "Last Session"

RCA (BLUEBIRD) AXM2-5501 - Tampa Red "Guitar Wizard"

RED LIGHTNING RL 005 - "Blues In D Natural" (British import)

REPRISE MS 2052 - Ry Cooder "Into The Purple Valley"
MS 2089 - John Fahey "Rivers and Religion"
MS 2117 - Ry Cooder "Boomer's Story"
MS 2179 - Ry Cooder "Paradise and Lunch"
RS 6402 - Ry Cooder "Ry Cooder"
2RS 6482 - John Renbourn "John Renbourn"

REVIVAL RVS 1001 - Fred McDowell and Johnny Woods (English import)

ROLLING STONES COC 59100 - Rolling Stones "Sticky Fingers"

ROOTS RL 324 - Blind Willie McTell (1929 - 1935)
RL 328 - "Southern Sanctified Music" (Various Artists)
RL 332 - "Cream Of The Crop" (Various Artists)
SL 504 - "The Vocal Intensity Of Son House"

SIRE SES 97003 - "The 1968 Memphis Country Blues Festival" (Various Artists)

SUE 918 - "Best Of Elmore James" (British import)
927 - "Elmore James Memorial Album (British import)

SUNNYLAND KS 100 - "Vintage Muddy Waters" (English import)

SYMPOSIUM 2001 - Leo Kottke "Circle 'Round The Sun"

TAKOMA 1001 - Bukka White "Mississippi Blues"
1004 - John Fahey "The Dance Of Death and Other Plantation Favorites" - Vol. III
1008 - John Fahey "The Great San Bernadino Birthday Party" - Vol. IV
1020 - John Fahey "Christmas Album"
1023 - Eddie Jones and Edward Hazelton "One String Blues"
1024 - Leo Kottke "6 and 12 String Guitar"
1028 - Fred Gerlach "Songs My Mother Never Sang"
1034 - Peter Lang "The Thing At The Nursery Room Window"
1040 - Leo Kottke, Peter Lang and John Fahey
9015 - John Fahey "Transfiguration Of Blind Joe Death" - Vol. I

TESTAMENT 2207 - Johnnie Shines and Muddy Waters "Chicago Blues"
2208 - Fred McDowell "My Home Is In The Delta"
2210 - Muddy Waters "Down On Stovall's Plantation" (1941 - 1942)
2212 - Johnnie Shines "Masters Of The Modern Blues - Vol. 1"
2213 - J. B. Hutto "Masters Of The Modern Blues - Vol. 2"
2215 - Robert Nighthawk "Masters Of The Modern Blues - Vol. 4"
2217 - Johnnie Shines with Big Walter Horton
2219 - Fred McDowell "Amazing Grace"
2221 - Johnnie Shines "Standing At The Crossroads"

TRADITIONAL SR 372 - Sparky Rucker "Bound To Sing The Blues"

TRANS-ATLANTIC 194 - "Fred McDowell In London - Vol. 1" (Import)

TRIP 8007 - "History Of Elmore James"
9511 - "History Of Elmore James - Vol. II"

VANGUARD VSD 1/2 - "Best Of Chicago Blues"
VSD 25/26 - "Great Bluesmen"
VSD 55/56 - "Essential John Fahey"
VSD 79145 - "Blues At New Port"
VSD 79198 - John Hammond "Country Blues"
VSD 79216 - "Chicago - The Blues Today"
VSD 79217 - "Chicago - The Blues Today - Vol. 2"

WARNER BROS. BS 2643 - Bonnie Raitt "Give It Up"
BS 2729 - Bonnie Raitt "Taking My Time"
WS 1953 - Bonnie Raitt "Bonnie Raitt"

YAZOO 1001 - "Mississippi Blues" (1927 - 1941; Various Artists)
1005 - "Blind Willie McTell - The Early Years" (1927 - 1933)
1009 - "Mississippi Moaners" (1927 - 1942)
1016 - "Guitar Wizards" (1926 - 1935)
1020 - "Charlie Patton - Founder Of The Delta Blues"
1026 - "Country Blues Bottleneck Classics"
1937 - "Blind Willie McTell - Vol. 2"
1039 - Tampa Red "Bottleneck Guitar" (1928 - 1937)

A cassette tape with most of the songs from this book is available. The publisher strongly recommends the use of this cassette along with the text to insure accuracy of interpretation and ease in learning.

If the cassette was not included as part of a book/cassette package, it is available from:

SUNNY MOUNTAIN RECORDS, INC.
P.O. Box 14592, Gainesville, FL 32604

or

MEL BAY PUBLICATIONS, INC.
P.O. Box 66, Pacific, MO 63069-0066

ALPHABETICAL SONG INDEX

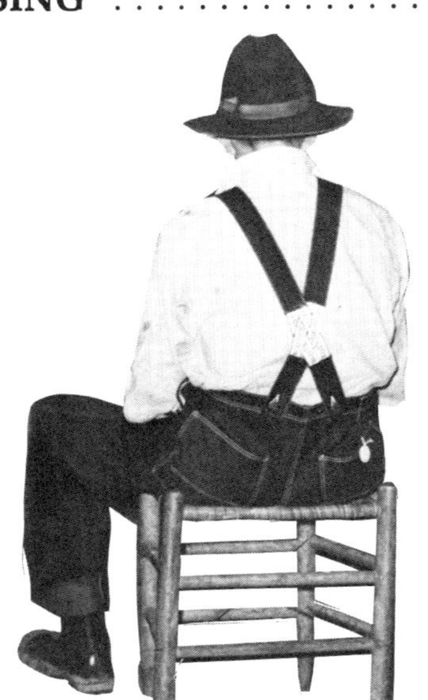

Library of Congress Collection

THE END